DESPISING THE SHAME

by

Talia Stone

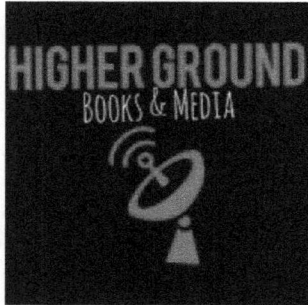

Higher Ground Books & Media
Springfield, Ohio.
http://www.highergroundbooksandmedia.com

Printed in the United States of America 2020

DESPISING THE SHAME

by

Talia Stone

To R, Dr. Cole, and Benny.

Thank you for your enduring help.

"Only the truth is kind."
— Maj Ragain

"Do not participate in the unfruitful deeds of darkness, but instead even expose them; for it is disgraceful even to speak of the things which are done by them in secret. But all things become visible when they are exposed by the light, for everything that becomes visible is light. For this reason, it says:

Awake, sleeper,
And arise from the dead,
And Christ will shine on you."

— St. Paul, Book to the Ephesians

REVIEW

Everyone, but especially every man, should read this book. I think many of us are in denial (or simply clueless) about just how hazardous it can be to live as a woman in this society. Even as a fairly liberal man myself, I truly had no idea about the prevalence and impact of sexual abuse until very recently.

In Despising the Shame, Talia tells the story of her experience of (and recovery from) sexual abuse, addiction, and betrayal. I found many of the episodes painful to read because they were told with such terrifying realism. Yet, none of what is written is for shock value. Instead, the matter-of-fact, "this is just what happened" nature of the reporting makes the book that much more poignant. I'm unsettled by what I've read in Despising the Shame, and that's a good thing.

But this isn't just a book about sexual abuse. It's a raw and candid exploration of psychology, spirituality, and redemption. Written with so much dexterity, Talia traverses the internal terrain of one who has experienced deep trauma and found the grace of healing. She cautions us all against the "snakes in the grass" that can seek to derail this process--especially the empty pseudo-spirituality of so-called "gurus" who are quite often predators seeking to devour their would-be prey. As a former pastor, I'm grateful for her cautionary tales about the ways churches and religious leaders can harm and re-traumatize victims.

Ultimately, though, Talia is not a victim. She has rejected the shame that kept her imprisoned and has found the peace of God's love and acceptance of Christ's sacrifice. As painful as it was to read this book, it gave me so much hope. I'm grateful for Talia Stone's courageous decision to share her story.

-- Beau Brown, author of No More Churches

Chapter One

*"Indeed, I have sinned against the Lord God of Israel, and this is
what I have done."*
(Joshua 7:20)

I met a man God loved. He wanted to be remembered. I remember
what he taught me about good and evil. I remember what I learned
about God.

The first time I heard about him, I was sitting on my
neighbor's dock. My husband and I had just bought a beautiful two-
story home overlooking a small lake on the edge of town. This
reservoir provided a perfect escape for a mermaid like me. I had
preferred water to land since I first discovered it, spending every
summer smelling of chlorine and aloe and welcoming the tan lines
that coincided with my transfiguration into a water creature who
could break free of the mayhem above and sojourn to the tranquility
beneath the surface. The top of the tall, tan house was lined with
windows from end to end, welcoming the natural light into the lofts
tucked away in the uppermost corners, and behind the stained-glass
window of the east wall was a large bedroom with a cathedral ceiling
and a balcony, providing a view of a silver maple adorned with
sparkling fishing lures left behind by the miscasts of local fishermen.
The neighborhood held a feeling of self-containment that brought me
peace. It was my oasis. I imagined myself safely dwelling in a
simulacrum of the tiny snow globe that I used to shake as a child,
watching the snow swirl about in that miniature world. Except, in
my real-world globe, it was summer. The sun shone on my face. The
water beckoned me. I had no way of knowing my globe was about to
be turned upside down, that the violent shaking would bring me to
my knees. Sitting under a canopy of stars, drinking a cold can of
beer with my new neighbors, I had my first introduction to the man
who would insist that I remember him. One of my neighbors told me
that the old, run-down cabin next to my house was owned by an 88-
year-old woman who still came back to stay in the cabin every
summer.

"Her son comes, too," she said. "He's always lying on the
porch with a book or working on his poetry. He's really smart."

She continued to speak of him with admiration and respect.

He loved his mother. His wife sometimes accompanied him to the cabin. It was obvious she held this man in high esteem. I found myself developing reverence for him just by hearing about him.

"He's crippled though," she added. "He had polio as a kid."

And so, Major Dan Ragain entered my consciousness. Despite how it sounds, his first name did not refer to a military rank. It was the name his mother had chosen for him at his birth, a name that means *greater*. He was well-known, both in the lakeside community I had joined and at a university 500 miles away where he had been decorated as the "father of poetry." Everyone called him Maj, pronounced *mage*, which is fitting. He was not only full of poetry, but also teachings of wisdom, and as my neighbor had so aptly pointed out, *smarts*. In a word, he carries *magic*, just as his nickname implies. I heard only good things about him from my new community within the oasis-like globe. He was a professor in an eastern college town where he had made his home. He lent compassion to combat veterans, helping them heal. He was also a great fisherman, and all the men in the neighborhood were eager to gather around to hear his old stories, learn how to tie a blood knot, or hear a clever joke. There seemed to be no end to his patience, kindness, and empathy. By the time I met him face-to-face, my deference for him had already been well-formed.

When I first saw him, he was lying on his belly on the front porch of the same cabin where he had spent summers as a young boy. Though unable to walk, he was rarely coupled with his wheelchair, preferring instead to sit or lie on the ground. He used his upper-body and the strength of his arms to move about as he dragged useless legs behind. A white mustache and matching soul patch framed his mouth. At first sight, he was older than I had imagined, appearing before me as a venerable grandfather any girl would readily admire. Beneath his stonewashed denim pants, his legs were withered, but his alluring aura transcended the atrophy of his body.

Already, I had spent the previous month growing to love his mother, who had arrived at the lake weeks before her son, still finishing his work at the university before the summer break. She and I bonded quickly: spending evenings on her porch and sharing stories about our lives. Hers were always about the pride and joy who would soon lay on the porch before me, unable to stand upon two shrunken legs. To her, he would always be her son of misfortune, stricken with polio as a child, but despite that, would still grow into the fullness of adulthood. Even though sixty years had passed, she saw still her eight-year-old child, and through her eyes, I saw that, too. Crippled innocence. A mother's son.

I've heard that to a mother, a son is never a fully-grown man, and likewise, a son is never a fully-grown man until he understands and accepts this about his mother. She had lost her younger son to an automobile accident in his youth, so Maj was her only surviving child. He was her world. As we approached him for the first time, Maj looked up at my husband and me from the ground as we exchanged smiles, then names. His calmness and composure were contagious. His words soothing and well spoken. As I stood with him, making our first introductions to each other, the neighbors of the wooded community where my husband and I had made our new home began to assemble in reverence, drawn into the spiritual circle Maj creates, one by one. It was as if homage was being paid to our seasonal neighbor from the east. I was beginning to understand why. It just felt good to be around him.

My husband and I walked the short path back to our home, leaving the neighbors with their visiting guru. Later, as I wandered alone down the private road of my newfound paradise, Maj called to me. He wanted to give me a book of poetry he had written called *A Hungry Ghost Surrenders His Tacklebox*. On the cover is a pen sketch of an old, bearded man, sitting naked on the top of a rock, his scrawny legs open wide and without shame. He holds in his hands a bent bow, string drawn tightly toward his chest, with a heavy-headed arrow aimed purposefully for the heavens. It is a fisherman's book, written by a well-practiced angler. As he presented the gift to me, he opened it to the inside cover and sketched a watering can with flowers blooming from the top before inscribing with wet, black ink, "Welcome to the neighborhood." As I stood, I watched his aged and crooked hands holding the pen with an inspiring sort of persistence that could not be dominated by the affliction that I now understood not only shriveled his legs and left him on his belly, but also had affected most of his body, down to the fingertips. At last, he signed his name, *Maj*, and looked up at me with a grin as he handed me his heart, bound in a 200-page paperback. A seed was planted.

My first summer in the globe came and went. I was learning about love. I loved Maj's mother and was enamored by the love she felt for her boy. Washington Irving wrote in his story about the widow and her son, "There is an endearing tenderness in the love of a mother to a son that transcends all other affections of the heart." I saw this in her love for Maj, and soon I would come to feel it, too.

Just before spring arrived, I became pregnant with a baby boy. The globe now held an added measure of hope and expectation. I pictured my son someday learning to swim in the cool waters of the gentle lake, climbing the ladder of the loft, scooting down the spiral staircase, and building blanket forts by the warm, crackling fireplace. That fall, he came forth in blood, water, and pain. The umbilical cord had snaked its way around his neck, threatening to snuff out what had been created inside me, but life prevailed and love was born. Still, I was terrified.

I named my son Abram, *exalted father*.

Chapter Two

*"Do not call anyone on earth your father; for One is your Father,
He who is in heaven."*
(Matthew 23:9)

Later I would have to ask myself why I named my child *dad*. A
father is the first man with whom a little girl falls in love. We carry
these childhood constructs of our daddies with us our entire lives.
My daddy was fighting demons. He was raised a Catholic boy and
got drunk on the leftover communion wine. He experimented with
drugs until the drugs started experimenting with him. My very first
memory is of seeing a single tear roll down his cheek the day his
mother died. I was only three, and until then, I had never known that
there were things in the world that could make my father cry. When I
was in fifth grade, he lost a well-paying job because he was using
methamphetamine. His unemployment made it impossible for my
parents to continue to send me to the private, Christian school I had
attended for six years, and I was thrust awkwardly and suddenly into
public school, where I was surrounded by strangers. During those
days, I spent most nights listening to my parents yell back and forth
at each other from the kitchen adjacent to my bedroom. The bottle
kept him away from me, and the screaming kept me away from him.
Though we lived under the same roof, I felt abandoned.

But I never stopped looking up to him. He may not have been
able to walk straight, but he was leading me. He was all I knew.
From him I was learning how to be loved and protected. I accepted
whatever he could offer, and I longed for the rest of it. I needed him.

When I entered the halls of that junior high in sixth grade, I
needed him. When the shin-length skirts that were required in my
Christian school were suddenly traded for a short cheerleading skirt
that I didn't even want to wear, I needed him. When the friends from
my Bible school were replaced with bullies who pushed me into
trash cans in the hallway and followed me from the cafeteria to the
bathroom where they threw food on me, I needed him. When a boy
tried to unbutton my jeans and reach down my pants, I needed him. I
wonder what he needed that he didn't get, what emptiness he was
trying to fill with drugs and booze.

Now I had a child of my own, and I had never wanted to
protect anything more than I wanted to protect him. I was crushed

beneath the fearful weight of failing him, of being a bad mother. With the trauma of his birth, all of my past traumas began to surface and threatened to extinguish me. I had not succeeded at protecting myself, how could I protect him? There were family secrets lurking in the dark corners of my mind. Freud wrote that unexpressed emotions never die. They are buried alive and will come forth later in uglier ways. It was about to become ugly.

I couldn't conceal my sudden anxiety and depression from my midwife at the appointments following Abram's birth. She quickly diagnosed postpartum depression and offered a prescription to improve my mood. As she spoke of how overwhelming it can be to keep up with the laundry when caring for a newborn, her words faded into the background while I visited the memory of the real problem in my mind's eye. Winter came, and the antidepressants weren't helping. Soon, I developed a respiratory infection and bought an over-the-counter cough medicine to help me sleep at night. I took both my prescribed antidepressant and the cough medicine before bed, hoping to get a couple of hours of sleep before I nursed my son again. To my surprise, I felt better, but I could not sleep. I had energy, and my mood improved. I was relieved to feel better, and the lack of sleep didn't seem to be such a problem.

Soon, the cough was gone, but the cough medicine wasn't, and I kept taking it. I didn't know that I was high. Maybe I had been so low that "high" felt normal. Unbeknownst to me, the unlucky combination of cough medicine with my antidepressant was releasing floods of serotonin into my brain. When I needed to take more than the bottle recommended in order to feel better, I knew there was a problem, and I became aware that I was living with a perpetual buzz. Through all this, winter passed. Spring came and went. The drug was numbing me from the pain of my secret, so I kept my new addiction a secret so that I could continue to keep the secret of the family. It worked for a while, until I became so numb that I finally allowed myself to speak.

My behavior became so erratic one day that my husband called my mother to our house. I was out of touch with reality. I was climbing on the kitchen counters. I was hallucinating yet asking if I made sense to them. My husband, trying so hard to be reassuring, said that he understood me. It was then that I sat down on the dining room floor and pulled my knees to my chest. As I rocked back and forth in a desperate attempt to comfort myself, I looked at my mother and my husband and began chanting.

This started with him. This started with him. This started with him ...

The expressions on their faces were identical, marked by both fear and denial, as they simultaneously reminded me not to talk about *that*. The straight jacket I had been wearing for years tightened around my chest, my arms, my throat. *Don't talk?* That is precisely what I had been doing for years. I obeyed them in the midst of my nervous breakdown. I stood and walked to the corner of the living room to look out across the lake through the bay window framing the water, and a noise that I did not recognize escaped my throat. It was a guttural howl, sounding more animal than human. I didn't realize it was coming from me until my husband grabbed me by my shoulders and spoke firmly, "Pull yourself together."

At that very moment, my son let out a cry. In the climax of my desperation, a love that hid deep within me brought silence, and I went to my son. My mother left the house. My husband left the room. But the distraction from pain that I found in that moment of deep repression as I tended to my child could not last forever. Later that night, I had a seizure. As a result of the cocktail of drugs I had been taking, an excess of serotonin had developed in my body, and I experienced the symptoms of serotonin syndrome. Left untreated, it can be fatal. My husband once again contacted my mother, and they agreed that I needed to get help. They wanted my drug problem to be under control. In the morning, I contacted a psychologist's office, and the secretary who took my call asked what sort of help I was seeking. Confounded, I returned to the mute state I had practiced for eight years, imagining the looks on the faces of my husband and mother when I had broken my vow of silence the day before.

The pause was too long, and she broke the silence by asking, "Is it a marital problem?" I quickly confessed that I had a drug problem, and she said that she would talk to the psychologist and call me back. As I hung up the phone, wild noises escaped my vocal cords once more, and my husband came running to ask what had happened.

"She knew nobody could ever want to be married to me!" I wailed.

The next week, I walked into the waiting room of a shrink, feeling both like I shouldn't be there and that I might be completely crazy. I distracted myself by examining the walls of the waiting room. A small, white frame hanging on the wall behind the secretary's desk bordered the words: *It's been said that time heals all wounds. But it's good to remember, that it also cures concrete.*

Suddenly, a man opened the door and welcomed me into his office. I was caught off-guard by his presence. I had expected someone more imposing, more formal, but he was not that. He wore a button-up shirt, but no tie or jacket. His demeanor was welcoming and comfortable. While sitting in the waiting room, I had been preparing for a meeting with an authoritative know-it-all, but the man who had revealed himself quickly let me know, without even saying it, that he was someone who was capable of listening. I stood awkwardly, my eyes passing over the knick-knacks and shelves of books, a picture of an eagle, and coming to rest on one of the many statues of a wolf that decorated his office. I looked at the couch against the back wall and a recliner of such deep maroon that it seemed purple.

"Where do I sit?" I asked nervously.

He smiled and said, "Wherever you'd like."

I sank into the overstuffed purple chair with my head down and studied him from the corner of my eye. He introduced himself with the same name as my father.

"What's with all the wolves?" I asked.

He looked into my eyes and said, "My name means *protecting wolf-shield.*"

I made the decision in that moment to never tell him that he shared my father's name. My father had not lived up to his responsibility of protector, and I needed this man to be different. He asked how he could help me. I had been anticipating this moment and knew I wouldn't be able to speak. Opening my green leather journal, I pulled back the ribbon bookmark to find the page where I had written what I could not say and held the journal toward him. He looked at me and then looked down at the journal. Slowly, he leaned forward and took the book into his hand. I watched him closely as he read the words I had written:

I believe in God. There is a sinful incident in my past. I feel guilty. I am afraid of being abandoned or betrayed. I believe this all to be a spiritual battle.

He looked up and found my eyes again. "Ok," he said as he handed my journal back to me. "What is the sinful incident in your past?"

I tried to tell him. God knows I tried. I tried to tell him about the walk I didn't want to take, the car ride, waking up with him on top of me and inside me.

The next thing I knew I was floating above the chairs in the room where I was seated with this new and unfamiliar man, my therapist, when I suddenly heard him coaching me, "Have you ever played a wind instrument? Blow the air out of your mouth. Now, take a deep breath through your nose."

When I finally caught my breath, I looked down, and I noticed that I was curled into a ball on the cushion of the chair. He observed the position of my body, saying, "Your arms are crossed over your chest. You are squeezing your legs together, and you are in the fetal position. You are trying to protect yourself."

I couldn't remember what had just happened.

"You dissociated," he said. "That sinful incident in your past is called *rape*."

I became nauseous and felt like ice was running through my veins. He quickly stood and poured me a glass of water. We sat quietly for a while. I had done all that I could do for that appointment, and he knew it.

As the hour came to a close, he said with certainty, "You are not hopeless or helpless, and I will not abandon you. How often may I see you?" We decided on once a week, and I left the office that had quickly become my sanctuary.

I returned to the globe. The tall house. The lake. The blue sky was filled with fluffy, white cumulus clouds, softening the ceiling of my sphere of safety. Summer had returned. So had Maj and his mother. I proudly presented my son to them, a baby boy I loved with every part of my mind, body, and soul. In that moment, a family began to grow. Maj's mother had never recovered from the tragic loss of her son, ripped from this world in a car accident when he was only eighteen years young. She reveled in the opportunity I was giving her to know Abram. She saw a younger version of herself in me as she watched my son and I begin our lives together on the very front porch where she, too, had raised a son. Two sons. Her son also welcomed me closer, adopting me into his family.

One afternoon he told me, "You are the daughter Mcm never had, the one she has so needed. I told her this afternoon in a long, relaxed conversation that you pray for her and love her. I told her that she has a daughter now."

I smiled at the thought. *Did that make Maj my brother?* I have only one sister. She was my best friend once upon a time, and I missed her every day.

He continued, "Do continue to hold Mom in your circle. That is so important, and you are in a position to do that. It anchors her to her life at the lake, to a life she loves. You and she fill something in each other. Love. A beautiful story."

I thought of the watering can he had drawn on the book he gave me. Surely the seed that had been planted that day was being watered throughout this second summer as love for my new neighbors grew in my heart.

The solstice of summer passed, but I continued to bask in the refuge I had found in people. My psychologist, who I decided to address by his initial "R" rather than call him by my own father's name, provided the support and guidance that I could not obtain from my family, or sadly, my husband. Though he was a kind man and a good friend, my husband was unable to confront my past with me. He supported my decision to go to therapy and saw that Maj also offered guidance and direction as he appointed me an honorary member of his family. My husband thanked him for his kindness. The inclusion into a new family was heartening as my place in my own family had been dashed and divided in the blizzard of a snowstorm that threatened to blow away the last foundations of the home that we had been trying, and failing, to make together. There was a reason I had sought a new globe to shelter me. Since then, I had developed a chameleon soul willing to attach myself to anyone who would assume me. I remember the moment when I thought that my husband was the right man to marry. He had just said, "I don't think that either of us need to talk about our sexual history to each other." Relief swept over me.

When I was seventeen years old, my sister's fiancé raped me. This was the secret that my mother and husband reminded me to keep in the dark. This was the memory that so frightened me that I disconnected from my body and hyperventilated as I tried to recall the details at my first therapy appointment. This was the source of trauma that disqualified me from ever receiving help from my family. Never before had I so identified with the Christ who uttered, "Father forgive them, for they know not what they do."

Chapter Three

"He took hold of her and said to her, 'Come, lie with me, my sister.'"
(II Samuel 13:11)

The night that changed my life forever started with Captain Morgan and a movie. My sister and her fiancé brought both into my bedroom and invited me to spend the evening with them. My sister was my closest companion, and I enjoyed any opportunity to spend time with her. She had met the man she would later marry when they were both fifteen. Everyone thought they were destined to be together. They were even born on the same day, in the same hospital. I was 11 when they started dating, and my sister was painting a picture for me of what a relationship with a man could be. I watched their romance develop over six years, and they talked openly about getting married. He proposed to her when they were preparing to leave high school and begin college. Though he would not become my brother-in-law until much later, by the age of seventeen I could conceive of no other way to think of him. He had been a brother to me.

After a movie that I can't remember because of too many rum and Diet Coke cocktails, a pizza, and hushed conversation so as not to draw the attention of my mother, a bigger, more surreptitious drama began to unfold than could ever be captured on the silver screen. My sister fell asleep, and her fiancé asked me to go on a walk with him to the railroad tracks near my home. This had happened before. On a previous walk to the overpass, he had told me that he had been thinking. Perhaps he could just be friends with my sister. That he had feelings for me. I told him that it could never happen, and he replied, "I was so excited to talk to you about this, and now I feel like I want to die."

As he propositioned me for another trek to that landmark of crisis, I became anxious and refused. I didn't want to do anything to hurt my sister. He poured more drinks in the safety of my bedroom, where my sister lay sleeping, and my parents were lying in bed on just the other side of the wall. My underaged body became intoxicated, and I have a vague memory of him saying that we should go jump on the trampoline in his parent's backyard. I don't remember getting into his car, but I recall the wet grass beneath my feet when I got out of the car at his house. Under a veil of darkness, we crossed the yard and climbed onto the trampoline. As we were jumping, he was reaching for me and touching me, and I became very nervous. I told him that I was uncomfortable, that my socks were wet, and that I was ready to go. He offered to get me dry socks before we left and led me into the dark house. Every light was off. His parents were asleep down the hall. I sat on the edge of his bed to wait while he found the socks. It is here that my memory fails me. Either my mind has subdued the image of him approaching me, or I had blacked out. My memory awakens only with the weight of his body covering me as he took something I had not offered.

I was overwhelmed, petrified, able only to utter one word of protest. *Don't.* My mind searched for a way to cope with the change that was occurring inside of me. It was as if a butterfly was becoming a caterpillar. A regression of mind and spirit. A reverse metamorphosis that would threaten to annihilate me. When it was over, I went to the door, and as my hand touched the knob, I began to cry. He covered my grief with his hand. I returned to my bedroom that night a different person. Gone was the girl who could laugh openly and abide with others in the absence of fear. Any sense of value that I had before began to dissipate. I was closed now. He told me not to tell. I felt guilty for keeping the secret. I knew my sister would be hurt by what had happened, and as much as I wanted to tell the truth, I could not bring myself to inflict pain on her. So, my obedience to a man who had hurt me took root. I became mute. I was owned by what I could not say. What I hid controlled me. I became a slave to the secret. Later, he told me that guilt was a fruitless emotion because it never really turned into anything else. Mine did. In the dark recesses of my mind, my guilt grew, and I wrapped myself in shame. I became angry about the way that I felt. Surely someone needed to be punished for this atrocity.

The first time I cut myself was after I had told a boy who liked me that I had been raped. Ever since that fateful night, I had been haunted by the thought of never finding a partner who would accept me after knowing that the man who would become a member of my family had invaded me in the worst way. But here was a boy offering to love me, so I tried to overcome my fears and told him the truth. Still, my apprehension was justified when the boy who had said he liked me didn't become angry at the man who violated me. Instead, he flew into a jealous rage and condemned me. As he walked down my parent's driveway and left, I walked to the silverware drawer in the kitchen and slid the blade of a paring knife across my left arm. This became my method of atonement. It proved to be a penance that was difficult to break. Months into my therapy with R, I was still showing up with bleeding arms and scabs.

I continued therapy with R, who diagnosed me with post-traumatic stress disorder and walked with me as I began the difficult process of defining who I was and how the past would affect me. I could sense myself becoming dependent on my interaction with him and told him that I was scared. He assured me that just as a small child who is learning how to walk looks back to make sure that her parents are still near, so would he remain close by as I learned to find my balance on my own two feet. I had faith in God. I was one of those girls with that old-time religion planted in her heart. I sensed a freedom from torment that was available if only I could grasp it, but I demanded punishment for the sin that had taken place. The crossfire of spiritual warfare ensued.

Chapter Four

*"For though we walk in the flesh, we do not war according to the
flesh."*
(II Corinthians 10:3)

Maj offered his help. He knew that I was in therapy, but I hadn't yet
told him why. He was leaving the lake for the summer and heading
back to his home in the east, but he began writing letters to help me
sort through my problems. He was no stranger to post-traumatic
stress. He told me that in the town where he lived he facilitated a
poetry circle for veterans suffering from the same psychological
affliction that I was experiencing. Maj created an outlet for these
traumatized veterans to be able to express themselves, to heal from
the fear that continued to consume them even though the immediate
danger had passed.

I began to hope that he would be able to help me if I ever told
him of the circumstances in my family and why his welcoming me
into his family had warmed my heart. In fact, I was beginning to feel
compelled to share with him because of how generous he was being
toward me. Still, I withheld what I thought would be a burden to
him. I bid him and his mother farewell and looked forward to the
following summer when I would see them again.

As fall approached, I trudged forward in my despondency,
believing that for now R could help me, and hoping that maybe one
day I would have the courage to trust others. R did help, but I had
stopped eating. Throughout the fall and winter, I nurtured my son
and punished myself. We were both learning how to walk. I was still
living in the fear of failing in my responsibility of motherhood. My
husband and I held his hands as he tottered around, exploring the
world. When not in the sanctuary of therapy, I looked back at R for
reassurance as I tried to learn to walk in the world with all of the fear
and distrust that I was carrying. R helped me see that I needed to be
able to look at danger and study it, but not to be afraid. One evening
as I sat in his office, amidst the smell of coffee and comforted by the
wolf figurines that now symbolized the shrink who was becoming
my shield, he said to me, "When you are walking through the jungle,
you see the snakes, you know they are there, and you don't let them
bite you, but you don't let them stop you from walking." I was

determined to do this. I had spent so long being closed off from everyone in the silence of my secret, but R had shown me that he would not abandon me because of my hurt and that it was indeed possible for me to trust others.

Learning to trust, I reached for the hand of the man who couldn't walk. Like R, he was becoming a father figure to me. He encouraged me, sending me letters through the "snail mail" that he loved so much. He treasured real paper folded up in envelopes that you can hold in your hands. Messages scribbled in ink-formed letters that show the fingerprints of the people who formed them. The written word. He taught me that spiritual connections are fostered that way, and I welcomed that as I studied God's written word and prayed for answers and discernment. I shared Maj's letters and what I was learning from him with my husband. But the frequency of our correspondence increased, and eventually the snail mail turned into email as Maj wanted to show me that while he had gone the five hundred miles back to his fall, winter, and spring home, he was not away. He had left a piece of himself with me. He reminded me that just as we had spent many warm days under the sun on the lake, we both loved, we were now living under the same moon, even with the miles between us.

"That lake you love is special, it's full of Spirit," he wrote. I smiled when I read it, thankful for the Spirit Lake inside my globe that seemed to be growing more beautiful with every passing day. Maj said that I was, too. He said that I was a rosebud coming into bloom. Just after his compliment, I came across a quote by Anais Nin that read, "And the day came when the risk to remain tight in a bud was more painful than the risk it took to blossom." The synchronicity astounded me, and I was sure that R was right, I would soon be able to trust, and as Maj said, I would soon be able to bloom.

Although I believed that blooming was in my future, I was beginning to look like a wilted flower. My weight continued to drop as I added laxatives to my "diet." I covered the open wounds of my wrists with band-aids and began cutting on my ankles, and my socks were often soaked with blood. What should have been a colorful life was fading like a cut flower. Though I wanted to live more optimistically, I carried perpetually a sense of my own failure. I wanted to be able to trust again, but instead, I was dragging razor blades across my skin and starving myself. R saw through my pain.

He knew that I couldn't trust others because I couldn't trust myself. So, we unpacked the reasons for that. The follow-up trauma. The second rape.

Chapter Five

"However, he would not heed her voice; and being stronger than she, he forced her and lay with her."
(II Samuel 13:14)

When I was twenty-one, my closest friend wanted to celebrate her birthday in a big city. She recruited me to plan the event, complete with a limousine and fancy hotel, dinner at an expensive restaurant, and a group of friends. That kind of luxury was foreign to me, but I did my best to plan the celebration that she wanted. The weekend of her party came, and seven of her closest friends showed up for the festivities. The evening went well. Dinner was delicious, everyone was having a good time, and as I watched everyone dance and mingle, I was glad that she was having the fun weekend she had wanted.

Midnight passed and we returned to the extravagant hotel in the leather seats of our stretch limo. As we approached the hotel room that she and I were to share, she told me that she wanted to have sex with her boyfriend, so she asked me to sleep in one of the other rooms. Exasperated, I asked her where I was supposed to go, what I was supposed to do. "We paid for four rooms," she said. "Just stay in one of the other rooms."

I looked around at her other friends. One was a girl who was an acquaintance of mine, but she had brought her best friend from college with her, and they were heading to their room for the night. Two others were a boyfriend and girlfriend that I had never met before, and it was clear that they were closing the door to their room to do the same thing that my friend had in mind. The remaining partygoer was an ex-boyfriend of the birthday girl, a Marine from my hometown. He approached us as I was finishing my conversation with her.

"Seriously?"

I glared at her. I couldn't believe she was confronting me with this dilemma at the last minute, but I didn't want to ruin her day. More so, it was she who had paid for the hotel rooms and not me.

As he walked up to us, she asked him, "Can you two stay in a room together?"

"Sure," he said, nonchalantly.

I didn't want to stay in a room with him, but I had spent years trying to recover from my rape on my own, and much of that presented itself in an illusion of control that I attempted to maintain and a determination not to carry my experience with me into every other situation in my life. Namely, not to fear all men. Disappointed in my friend and in the situation, I pushed back the uneasiness I was feeling about agreeing to this. I looked at him and said, "Fine. If you can be a gentleman, we can stay in the same room. But keep your hands to yourself. One of us can sleep on the floor." He said that wouldn't be a problem, and we told my friend and her boyfriend goodnight before going to the room.

He was anything but gentle. I went to the bathroom and locked the door as I changed into a pair of sweatpants and did my best to prepare for a restless night of sleep. He got ready for bed while I was fidgeting with blankets and pillows, looking forward to resting after the long night. He was talking about the night we had at the restaurant and the dance club, and in a teasing way, he began commenting on how pretty I had looked that night. He said I wouldn't be bad "arm candy" for him.

I gave him a disapproving look just as he reached out and squeezed my hip. I backed away from him, but he tackled me onto the bed and started tickling me.

"Stop it," I told him.

He laughed and continued squeezing and tickling my stomach and hips, causing me to wiggle and flail on the bed.

"Knock it off, I'm serious," I said, more firmly.

His eyes changed from playful to intent, and he grabbed my right wrist with his left hand and pinned it to the pillow above my head. Using his other hand, he grabbed my remaining hand and last line of defense, forcing it over my head and onto the hand that had already been taken hostage. Reaching down with his right hand, he grabbed the waistband of my sweatpants and jerked them down in one swift motion. I was completely exposed as he reached into his own pants. I struggled against the muscular body of this attacking Marine to no avail. In a sudden moment of abhorrent pain, he invaded me. My power was gone.

As he thrust himself into me furiously, one more word pitifully escaped my lips.

"No," I whimpered.

He stopped. Just as painfully as he had stabbed me, he ripped himself out of me. I winced with his withdrawal.

"You're right," he said. "I should stop."

As he released my hands, I rolled to my side and ran to the bathroom, slamming the door and locking it. I stood by myself in horror and shock. I looked into the mirror, knowing that I could not assess my injury that way. Just then, I felt a trickle on my inner thigh. I looked down to see that he had not stopped because I said no--he had stopped because he was finished.

I felt contaminated. I sat on the floor and leaned against the toilet, with no trust that the lock on the bathroom door would keep me safe, with no trust that I could trust myself. I had gone into that hotel room even though I knew that I didn't want to be there. Look what that had cost me. A transaction had taken place, and the value within me that had been pierced four years earlier now seemed to have disappeared completely. I stood and unlocked the door. The lock wasn't protecting me anyway. I had learned that if a man wanted something, he would take it.

I walked from the bathroom and back into the room where he had just assaulted me. I knew I couldn't defend myself anyway. That had been clearly demonstrated.

"You raped me," I said.

"I know," he said flatly.

I walked past him and out the door into the hallway of the hotel and lowered myself to the rough carpet. My back curved, my head bowed, and my limbs bent as I drew them up to my chest. I returned to the position of a child in the womb trying to minimize my injury. But the damage was done.

Chapter Six

"For he who doubts is like a wave of the sea driven and tossed by the wind."
(James 1:6)

As spring approached, the blooming of the yellow tulips and Belladonna lilies began to reveal the lakeside garden in which I had been living the entire time. I tried to see myself as a flower bud germinating in the soil of the lessons I was learning from R and Maj, who had become established patriarchs in my life. But doubts about whether I would ever heal continued to plague me. Maj eased my mind, saying that "doubt fuels faith" and that he thought I was courageous. He added that my faith and earnest search for spiritual understanding were what drew him to me. He lived an open life, he said, and found it deeply nurturing that I was doing the same. R, too, told me that I was stronger than I could see and pointed out that my lack of trust for myself caused my distrust to unfold onto others and could keep even trustworthy people at a distance. I didn't want to be alone. He reminded me to reserve my childlike trust in God alone.

Then a storm hit. I had to go to Chicago for work. I was supposed to chaperone high school students on a three day-trip to various parts of the Windy City, but my problems began at the first rest stop along the way. I could not pee. I needed to. I wanted to. I tried to. But, I couldn't.

At the next rest stop, I tried again. Nothing. My medical doctor had prescribed Xanax to take in addition to my antidepressant, so I took my anti-anxiety medication in an attempt to relax enough to relieve myself. By the time I was able to call a cab and get to a Chicago hospital, it had been over twelve hours since I had urinated. The pain was dreadful. I was ushered into an emergency room where I had to spread my legs for a stranger in order to be catheterized. That level of vulnerability was at the bottom of my list of things I wanted to do that day, or any day. I turned my head from the nurse in humiliation as she inserted the tube. I found myself staring directly at a crucifix.

Later, I stood outside the hospital with a catheter inside of me and a bag of urine strapped to my leg as I held a cellphone to my ear talking to R. He said that he understood that I was likely having flashbacks of previous events and that he knew I was suffering. My husband had to drive five hours to Chicago in the middle of the night to bring me home. On the drive home, a friend sent me a text message, "Weeping may endure for the night, but joy comes in the morning." I wondered when my morning would come.

Back at the lake, I sought solace in another phone conversation with R. My boss wouldn't let me come back to work. They were forcing me to see a different counselor in order to get clearance that I was "fit" to return to work. The confidence I had been striving to develop was dwindling. I couldn't even go to the bathroom by myself. R was gentle and consoling. He told me that I was going to remove the catheter myself, that I could have control of that. Afterwards, he remained on the phone with me while I cried. I could hear the creaking of a rocking chair as he comforted me in silence. He couldn't take the pain away, but he could stay by my side, as he had promised he would. Much time passed while I sobbed, and he rocked. Not once did he mention ending the conversation. I felt accepted, understood, and loved. Finally, I told him I was going to hang up the phone. "Go to sleep," he said. I did.

Soon I awoke to another summer full of possibility with neighbors who had become family beside the waters of Spirit Lake. I thought of my paradisiacal globe as a garden filled with expectation and potential for healing. R told me I was going through a time of awakening. During this new dawn, he saw my hunger for the food I wasn't eating as my body began to look less like that of a new mother and more like that of a child, and he knew that my spirit was also searching for nourishment. I bought a new diary to journal what I was learning. The front was covered with sparrows, and in the corner were the words, "Joy comes in the morning." I believed the verse had meaning for my life and that one day I would look back at my weeping with a joyful heart. In the quiet of his office one evening, I passed my open journal to him. He leaned back in his chair and read these words aloud with awe, "Rich and powerful discoveries in Scripture await all of us, discoveries that are brand new, even from old, familiar passages." There was a long pause before he looked at me and smiled softly. "It's true," he told me.

Maj contacted me in preparation for the arrival of his family for the summer. I had become caretaker of the ramshackle cabin, the shabby temple that housed a family that was becoming my own.

Weeks before his arrival, he asked me to screw a lightbulb into a metal sconce on the kitchen wall and turn on the light. He said the flame would burn for us in the days leading up to his homecoming. I was delighted to do whatever he requested of me. I knocked down cobwebs, unlocked doors, and hung flowers and hummingbird feeders from the front porch where we would all gather. Maj's son and two pre-teen granddaughters would also visit this year, and I was eager to meet them and to observe the ever-widening circle of friends and neighbors present in my secluded universe.

Finally, the day came when our lakeshore community felt complete again. Maj and his wife joined his mother in the family cabin, followed days later by the appearance of his son and granddaughters. I treasured the chance to receive a glimpse of Maj in the role of father and grandfather. The family atmosphere deepened as we broke bread at backyard cookouts, swam in the muddy waters of the lake together, catfished off the pier, enjoyed front porch swinging at sunset, and star gazed until it was time to dream.

Having grown up in the same hometown into which I would be born 44 years later, Maj had long been a fixture of Spirit Lake. He had known some of the men in the neighborhood since their births. I became friends with Bradley, a strong young man of nearly sixteen, with a good heart and a willingness to help anyone in need. I bonded with Greg, a man from just down the road whose integrity I would come to respect and whose friendship I would cherish. This summer, I witnessed in Maj the skillful art of the knowledgeable fisherman as the three of them piled into a jon boat to trade stories and hunt bass. I savored the small tribe of men forming around me in the security of the village I had found.

Still, my swimsuit could not hide my trust issues and anguish, as my ribcage protruded from a malnourished body begging for absolution. Maj immediately noticed a drastic change in my appearance and inquired of its cause. In all my years of secrecy, neither friends nor family had ever recognized my suffering, or if they did, had never bothered to ask. Recalling my conversation with R highlighting the distrust that kept even trustworthy people at bay, I resolutely decided to share my secrets with the only family who seemed to care. I wrote a letter detailing the abuse that had transformed me into the outcast of my family and the degradation that occurred behind a locked hotel room door. I braced myself as I waited to see if summer would remain, or if once again, my globe would crack and shatter, hurling me into the blindness of a whiteout.

With the tenderness that I had hoped for, my wordsmith replied, "May your tears, may the words of your letter, join that river that, in turn, joins the great ocean of compassion. The enlightenment of the wave is to remember that it is water. When it crashes into the shore, its essential nature is not destroyed. It is still water. Only the form has changed. You and I are rocked in the cradle of that great ocean." Consolation for which I had waited an entire decade had finally arrived. He closed the letter, "I love you. I accept you fully."

Our conversations assumed greater direction as a result of my newfound trust, and I was grateful for his willingness to assuage my grief. He suggested that I disarm myself of self-imposed obstacles that were preventing my healing. Like R, Maj recognized that my hunger was an indication of a desire for something more than physical sustenance, he called this desire *yearning*. "Without great longing, nothing comes," he wrote. But he taught me that the first step is to empty one's self. Little did I know that when you empty yourself, you are preparing to be filled, whether you know it or not.

I longed for peace. I had felt it before. From birth to adulthood, I spent Sundays in the presence of God in the Bible-believing church that became not only my place of worship but also my childhood school and my home. In a world full of confusion, a red brick building with a sharp white steeple had always been my refuge. On a cold, January day when I was eight years old, the pastor of my church, who doubled duties as the principal of my school, lifted my small body from the water as I smiled and waved at my church family. On that day, I had been baptized in the name of the Father, Son, and the Holy Spirit. Twenty years later, I struggled to return to the peaceful innocence that I had experienced in simpler days.

I carried my son into my church community, doing my best to lead him into the knowledge of God. But my safe haven had been tainted. My brother-in-law had become a member of the church. I had long since realized that he had replaced me as the fourth member of my family of origin, but I refused to let him supplant me in the church family as well. His acceptance by my parents and sister had been my rejection. He was protected, so in turn, I wasn't. My mother adopted him as a son. My sister married him. My father walked her down the aisle. I watched, in a crimson maid of honor dress with a rosebud in my braided hair. If my parents had given me any birthright, it was in my church home, where my faith had formed, and I would not trade it for the world.

Chapter Seven

"Even my own familiar friend in whom I trusted, who ate my bread,
has lifted up his heel against me."
(Psalm 41:9)

My marriage was struggling as I wrestled with how to include my
husband in my broken life. I went to therapy alone. He was working
weekends to provide for our family, so I attended church without
him, too. He knew that I was in trouble, but he didn't know how to
help me. We agreed to seek help from our pastor, so on a Sunday
evening, I walked into his office and admitted to him and his wife
that my husband and I needed help. As he asked what was happening
within the marriage to cause problems, I tried to overcome my guilt
and told him that I had recently entered therapy after a period of
over-the-counter drug use In a particularly shameful moment of
decision, I also confessed that I had developed a drinking problem at
the age of seventeen that had lasted until I had seen the pink plus
sign appear on a home pregnancy test. He said, "Often people use
substances when there is something in their past that is bothering
them. Could there be something like that in your past?"

I started sweating. I wanted to be honest. I believed that I
should be. With shaking hands, I told him as much of the truth as I
could. "There was a sexual incident that took place. It's not easy to
talk about." I could not bring myself to tell him that a member of his
church had raped me. I still could not break the code of silence that
my family had instilled within me. I wanted him to ask me more
about what had happened, but he didn't. I left, having mentioned
only my own sins and being unwilling to say anything about the sins
of others.

I felt alone, surrounded by people in Sunday services with
whom I could not reveal my secrets. However, it happened that there
was one person in my church family who would be able to accept the
truth of what had happened to me, and we found each other in R's
office. We shared with one another the circumstances that had led us
to a sanctuary different than that of the church, one that allowed our
friendship to be based on truth and honesty. She was close friends
with our pastor's wife, and after my meeting with the pastor, the two
of them chose to discuss the details of my secret that I had shared
with each of them in confidentiality. I had trusted my friend with the

details of my story, and in trying to help, she uncovered that what had taken place was more than an *incident*. She told them that I had been raped and that the person who did it was someone they knew. She gave them his name. When I learned of this, I was disappointed that my confidence had been betrayed, but I chose to hope that some light, any light, would shine on the truth. However, a month later, my brother-in-law became a deacon of the church and my Sunday school teacher. Whatever efforts I had made to stand my ground somewhere, anywhere, had failed.

Though I had long been faced with the injustice of my situation, this betrayal of confidence followed by an ill-fated hope for some sort of help or retribution was too much to bear. The spiritual promotion of my brother-in-law nearly pushed me to the brink of sanity. I lamented to R about these events with my words and with my body. I stood at the cliff's edge, frail bodied with slashed and bleeding ankles, and I returned to drug abuse. The dextromethorphan found in cold medicines provided a numbing effect that I preferred over the thorniness of my unanesthetized feelings. I restricted myself to a bowl of cereal a day, eaten before bed, with two to four milligrams of Xanax to push me into sleep before I could be allowed the feeling of comfort from the food in my stomach. I asked R how people who claimed to love me could possibly exclude and abandon me the way my family had. How could the church look away from my suffering? He pursed his lips with inhibition that was uncharacteristic of him. R looked at me with sorrow in his eyes before he revealed a truth he knew would hurt, "They made you the sacrificial lamb."

That's the thing about sexual abuse. Nobody wants to look at it. Suddenly, the proverb to "see no evil, hear no evil, speak no evil" comes rushing to the defense of the onlookers in the form of denial. I suppose they feel that they have to make a judgment. They should. But I quickly learned that nobody wanted the responsibility.

Chapter Eight

"For nothing is secret that will not be revealed, nor anything
hidden that will not be known and come to light."
(Luke 8:17)

Years earlier, drowning in the guilt of transgression, I had wanted to
tell my sister what had happened. I also wanted help that I could not
receive without speaking. But the man who was as a brother to me
had sworn me to secrecy. I tested this once. I told my first boyfriend
in high school of what had happened during a phone conversation.
He broke up with me immediately, and I hung up the phone single
and with more than the ordinary angst of a girl who had been
dumped. I couldn't explain to anyone why I had suddenly been
rejected, but my sister's fiancé had an inkling. He called me, and as I
stood in the utility room of my parent's house, surrounded by dirty
laundry with the phone to my ear, he said, "I was afraid that would
happen. That was your relationship, but the relationship with your
sister is mine. It's my right to tell her, not yours."

Finally, the day came when he propositioned a way that he
might talk to my sister. Their engagement had lasted nearly seven
years, and it was obvious to me that he was not able to move forward
in marriage with a good conscience. I had started dating a baseball
player at the community college he and I were attending in my
hometown, and as our studies there were coming to an end, he
suggested I enroll in a university with him near his hometown, 1,000
miles away. My sister's fiancé said that he thought my absence
would provide a good opportunity for them to discuss both the
matter of marriage and the secret he had kept from her. I was ready
for the truth to be revealed, so I agreed.

The boy I was dating was not kind to me. My low self-worth
had manifested itself in a stereotypically abusive relationship
between a controlling guy and a girl lacking self-esteem. I moved
1,000 miles away from everything that I had ever known in order to
find closure. Full of anticipation, I spent two long summer months
abusing myself with whiskey in the heat of Texas until my cell
phone rang. I said hello and heard my sister's voice on the other end
of the line.

"He told me what happened," she said. I had waited so long
for this moment, yet I couldn't seem to remember how to breathe.

Her voice broke through the line again. "I don't know that I'll ever understand," she said. I was depleted of the emotional capacity to connect to her, of the words to express myself, of the ability to do anything more than collapse to the ground in exhaustion.

"I'm sorry," I whispered.

I can do nothing but echo my sister's sentiment. I'll never understand. I have no idea what he told her. Moving to Texas was nothing more than an instrument of resolution, so I returned home after I had been told that he had confessed to her. But it wasn't resolution to which I returned. I thought that I would find out what he had told her when I arrived, but instead I was informed of wedding plans. The date had finally been set, and it was less than six months away. I wondered what kind of parallel universe allowed these circumstances. Had my rape been acknowledged? Is that why we were celebrating? Had my sister told my parents? If so, were they going to ask me if I was okay? If not, was I allowed to ask them for help yet? Did my addiction to alcohol since the age of seventeen make sense to them now? Could they see the scars on my ankles as evidence of something real that needed to be addressed?

Over the next few months, I became dispirited as I realized that the answer to every single question was no. I stood at their Christmas wedding in the strapless crimson dress my sister had chosen for me, smiled for pictures, and listened as they promised to love each other until death. I didn't think things could get any harder, but at the continued festivities the day after the wedding, my sister's new husband came into an empty room where I had been standing alone. I turned my head and walked away from the smell of alcohol on his breath as he tried to kiss me. The trip to Texas had changed nothing, nor had a wedding, and it would be only two weeks until I attended another celebration, my friend's birthday at the hotel.

Chapter Nine

"How can a man be born when he is old? Can he enter a second
time into his mother's womb and be born?"
(John 3:4)

This sacrificial lamb thing. It's central to my story. To all stories. As
Maj and I grew closer, he stopped calling me by my first name, the
name that everyone else used to refer to the person they could see
and thought they knew. He called me by my middle name. *Talia*,
pronounced *tal-yuh*. It means *lamb of God*. Having him call me by a
new name highlighted the closeness that had developed, and I
embraced the possibility of a fresh start. I was willing to assume this
new identity while I sorted through the wreckage that had made me a
sacrificial lamb. When a crime is committed and judgment seems
imminent, people suddenly feel the pressure to choose a side. But
what will they put on the altar if they have to choose? If my sister
chose me, she would lose her high school sweetheart, her would-be
husband, her future children. If my mother chose me, she would
have to choose between the needs of her daughters and risk losing
the illusion of the happy family to which she clung. If my father
chose me, he would have to acknowledge that he had not protected
me in the first place. Because none of them were willing to make
their own sacrifices, they denied the truth and washed their hands.
But the truth remained, and I carried it, my body sagging beneath the
weight of a solitary burden. I accepted that I was the lamb.

It was easy for Maj to see that the lamb before him was
indeed a black sheep, wandering through a foggy pasture in search of
approval. As a child, I had always thought that my biological family
would love me unconditionally. The circumstances of my life were
not corresponding to that idea, and I became very disappointed. As I
sat on the cracked, concrete porch of the cabin with Maj before
another end of the summer departure, swatting mosquitoes and
gazing at the last light of the day streaming through the oak trees, I
said, "If the truth is what corresponds to the way things actually are,
then I am not fully accepted by my family. I can't be. They won't
even accept what happened."

I listened to the melodic chirping of crickets as he
contemplated my distress before instructing me with his deep,
gravelly voice, "Fully accept that disappointment, Talia. Stop

participating in their game of pretend." He looked up from his bony, folded hands and captured my eye with an unwavering intensity as he added, "Only the truth is kind."

Disappointment overtook me as I let his words sink into me. Just as I felt myself slipping into a pit of darkness, he threw me a rope, saying, "I remain a friend. That won't change."

I knew when Maj left that summer that he would continue to comfort me. As all the neighbors gave him goodbye hugs and handshakes, I knew that my correspondence with him would continue. Still, I would miss him. I bent down to the ground where he sat and wrapped my arms around the trunk of his body. He told me he could feel the sadness in my shoulders. I walked away, crossing the threshold from his yard to my own and took to my bed to cry.

In the shelter of my next appointment with R, he asked me why the tears were coming. "Because Maj had to go," I told him quietly. R smiled and said that my meeting Maj had been no coincidence. I held firmly to the assurance available through R's presence in my life. When times were hard, I needed only to remind myself of the quiet sanctuary of his office, not far from the dome holding the tall house and the shoddy cabin on Spirit Lake.

Times got hard. Again, I lost the ability to empty my bladder. In an attempt to avoid adding to my mounting medical bills, I went to a clinic and learned how to catheterize myself so that I could steer clear of the emergency room and the flashbacks I experienced by going there. Straight tip catheters became a regular item in my purse, and I was embarrassed that I couldn't do something as simple as take a piss. Times were hard for Maj and his mother, too. A couple of months after I told them goodbye, she fell and broke her wrist after receiving twilight sedation for a simple procedure. Shortly after that, she fell again and broke her hip. I was beside myself when Maj called to tell me that she was entering a nursing home. She was losing everything, her apartment, belongings, and car. Her freedom. I began calling her several times a week, and our connection strengthened as we comforted one another through difficult times.

Whispering to my mermaid heart, Maj wrote, "There's an old yoga practice I want you to try. Submerge yourself in Spirit Lake. Then swim, and as you do, inhale the emotions you are feeling and exhale the colors." I exhaled red and black and wondered what the colors meant. It wasn't a mermaid that Maj saw in me, though. Drawing from his Irish heritage, he told me that I was a mythological creature and introduced me to a legend from the folklore of his ancestors. I was a Silkie. Silkies are said to live as seals in the sea but shed their skin to become human on land. If a man can manage to steal the Silkie's skin, she is in his power and has no choice but to become his wife. They make excellent wives, but because their true home is the sea, they can be found gazing longingly at the ocean. I was mesmerized as I watched a movie about a mystifying and beautiful girl, Ondine, who gets caught in the net of a fisherman wading in the water. I identified with the story, as I sat on the edge of my pier dipping my tan feet into the water and staring out across the lake that was my home.

Perhaps my wish to live and float safely in the water was a conflict fundamental to the human condition. I wanted to grow on the land into the rose that Maj said I could become, but maybe a part of me wanted to return to the womb. I learned that nothing R said or did in therapy was without purpose. One evening as I took off my shoes and pulled my bare feet into the soft purple chair that I found comfort in every week, he told me that the color of the chair was no happenstance. It was representative of the womb where we all first find safety and security in our lives, before we are born. I had never considered this type of desire before, but I could see some relevance in it and began facetiously, but repeatedly, referring to R's office as my "womb room." Unfortunately, my womb room was about to be invaded by my own mother.

Chapter Ten

"All we like sheep have gone astray; we have turned, every one, to his own way; and the Lord has laid on Him the iniquity of us all."
(Isaiah 53:6)

Christmas was approaching, bringing authenticity to my fantasy of the snow globe, and I wanted to give a gift to the man who had shown me more of Christ than anyone ever had. The friend that I had found in his office and I went shopping in a dollar store for a small tree to decorate in his office. We contacted his secretary, whom I had grown to appreciate for her warm heartedness and understanding and arranged to show up with our gift while she was working, and he was gone. After chatting in the waiting room, we opened the door to the sanctuary and continued to talk and laugh lightheartedly as we hung glimmering, silver ornaments and blue tinsel from the little Christmas tree. I was feeling merry, something that I hadn't felt at Christmas in a long time.

As my friend and the secretary were applauding our work, I glanced over my shoulder at the chair of my protector. On a table next to his seat, my eyes caught a familiar sight. My mother's signature was at the bottom of a piece of paper resting on that table. I froze. As my therapy had progressed, it had become clear that my mother was nervous about what I was exposing there. This only added to my need for a place, and a person, that was safe. Therapy was my lifeline. It was the first time I had been able to receive help, and for an hour a week, evade the denial and attempts of my family to monitor the mouth that threatened to release my pain. I could not understand why she would show up in my psychologist's office without telling me. There was no good that could come from that. Several moments passed, and the secretary became aware of my disconnection as I stood, motionless. "Are you ok?" she inquired. I pointed at the paper, and she took a deep breath and turned the document face down. By this time, my friend was also asking if I were okay. I told them no, and that I needed to make a phone call. They looked worried as they stepped from the room and closed the door to give me privacy. I dropped into the womb chair and stared at the wall.

Reaching into my pocket for my phone, I dialed the number of the wolf who had protected me to find out if he were still the same

man, I had thought he was. "Hello?" his reassuring voice came
across the line.

"Hi, R. I'm in your office. We brought you a tree." He started
to thank me, but I cut him off. "I saw my mom's name in here. You
left a file out."

I heard him exhale before he asked, "What do you need from
me?"

I told him that I needed to know why, and I needed to know
what was going on. He told me he had to make one phone call, and
he would call me right back. I hung up the phone and lay my head on
the arm of the purple chair until my phone rang. "I called your
mother," he said. "I told her what you saw and asked her to sign a
release allowing me to talk to you about her appointment with me. I
told her that if she really wanted you to be okay, she'd grant that
permission." He promised me that we would deal with this at my
next appointment, and I left the conversation bewildered at her
motivation and angry that my sanctuary had been invaded.

We hold mothers to a high standard, sometimes expecting
perfection. My mother always told me that giving birth to me was
not that difficult. She just did it. It wasn't that painful. Perhaps I
should have expected her denial of my own pain. At my next
appointment, I learned that my mother had called R's office and
scheduled an appointment for herself without revealing her
relationship to me or her reason for coming. After she arrived, she
admitted her relationship to me, claimed that she wanted to help, and
expressed concern about distance that was growing between her and
me. As R realized that he was sitting with my mother, he said to her,
"If you are under the impression that I will speak to you about my
patient's therapy, you are mistaken." My mother defended her
reasons for being there, saying that she was unaware of some of the
troubles her daughter had experienced as a result of her husband's
alcoholism. She wanted him to know that she hadn't been the
problem. R suggested to her that if she were to enter therapy, it
should be to address the issues of her own life, and she left saying
that she might contact him for another appointment after the first of
the year. R immediately let me know that he had felt she would not
end up contacting him again, but if she did, he planned to refer her to
a colleague as it was a conflict of interest for him to consider treating
her. I felt betrayed. How could she not see that she could not help me
without first believing me?

Weeks after I had returned from Texas, I told my mother what had happened to me. I attempted to reach out for help. In the same kitchen where I had first spilled my own blood in atonement for what had taken place, I asked her if either my sister or my soon to be brother-in-law had informed her of the event. She mumbled that my sister had said that her fiancé and I had "gotten too close."

"Too close?" I stammered, incredulously. "It wasn't just--" I stopped myself before blurting out, "He did it." Embarrassed and ashamed, I hung my head and looked at her from the doorway, "*IT*, mom!"

She did something then that remains as a picture in my mind to this day. She covered her ears with her hands. Hear no evil. Then she said it, "I don't want to know, and I don't want to talk about it." Something inside of me broke. Maybe I had never accepted that the umbilical cord had long ago been severed, but I never realized until that moment that her mind was not capable of protecting me the way her body once had. Over the next several years, I told her many times that I had been raped. She never believed me.

The fear and overwhelming anger I felt following my mother's betrayal was intensified by my deepening sense of isolation during the holiday season. The hope, peace, and joy that I had been feeling as I decorated my therapist's office with the symbol of Christmas was replaced by despair, anxiety, and a deep sadness that I would never again know what it felt like to be loved by my family. Childhood memories of red bubble-lights on the green tree in front of my family's dining room windows, candy canes, meals at my grandma's house, cantatas at my church--all these seemed phantoms of an imagined past. But I was learning that I had a family that was not my family. Though I felt alone, I was not alone.

On Christmas Eve, Maj sent me a poem that ended with lines from a hymn I had learned in childhood:
Above thy deep and dreamless sleep
The silent stars go by.

Though I had lost my family, I had not yet lost Christmas. On Christmas Day, Maj reminded me, "Each day is a gift. Beneath the wrapping, there is a vast, inexplicable tenderness. Be alert to that."

I wanted to be alert to tenderness I could not experience from my family. Tenderness that I was receiving from both Maj and R. I continued my weekly pilgrimages to my only place of comfort, seeking help from the only person in my life who was able to see me, face-to-face, and receive me with compassion, respect, and truth. On the days when I could not go to therapy, I experienced the panic of a person fearing for her life. My attachment to him was a death grip that tightened each day until my next appointment. Somehow I struggled through the days between appointments until I could find relief in the sanctuary of his office, if only for an hour. He did not disappoint as he continued to guide me in ways that I would not understand until much later.

"Hey, doll!" he exclaimed one day as he opened his office door for me. He was always snacking during my sessions, picking through a combination of walnuts and apples, throwing the red apple slices away and eating the green ones. At this appointment, he cut into a block of holiday fudge, a Christmas gift from another patient. He gave me a large square and began eating his while we were talking. Every couple of minutes he urged me, "Eat some of your chocolate. Go ahead." I obediently took the smallest bite possible. Before much time had passed, he prompted me again. "Take a bite. It's good."

By the third time, I was frustrated. "I'll eat it when I'm ready, R! Back off a little."

He leaned back in his chair, looking impressed. "Very assertive. That was good. You should apply that kind of assertiveness to other areas of your life."

Initially, I couldn't help but be gratified by his compliment. I always wanted him to be proud of me. But as the lesson permeated my subconscious, I saw that he was providing a way for me to exercise my willpower that would not result in a famished body. On another occasion, I was caught off guard when he interrupted our dialogue to go to the bathroom. "Excuse me, I have to pee," he said, standing suddenly and leaving me alone in his office as he sauntered down the hall to the men's restroom. Therapy isn't cheap, and I was surprised that he wasn't willing to wait ten more minutes until the appointment was over. Ostensibly, he was just responding to a call of nature. In actuality, he was modeling for me the ability to empty my bladder when necessary, regardless of the situation. The instruction remained in the periphery of my mind, and I hadn't consciously reconciled what he was teaching me. Still, I duplicated the behavior.

A few weeks later, I stopped him mid-sentence, saying, "I

have to pee."

"Go, be good to your body," he encouraged. R knew how to talk to me. And I heard him, and responded, whether I was aware of it or not.

Maj, too, knew how to speak to me. He always told me that there was much that was hidden, but it was nearby. He shared some of it with me. He sent poems and introduced me to wise teachings that I had never before considered. A stanza from *The Rubaiyat* of Omar Khayyam was among his favorites. "Come, fill the Cup, and in the fire of Spring, Your Winter-garment of Repentance fling: The Bird of Time has but a little way to flutter--and the Bird is on the Wing." He said it was important that I consider this. I read everything he suggested, acclimating myself to the culture of poetry of which he was a part, as I absorbed the verses of "Eternity" by William Blake and Wendell Berry's "Do Not Be Ashamed." For my birthday, he sent another of the books he had authored. It was captivating to read stories of my erudite neighbor's life on the lake. It seemed destined that I had been blessed with a confidant who appeared in my own yard, like something was finally going my way. Someone finally chose me, with the ugliness of my abuse, and not only acted as if he loved and accepted me fully, but also told me that he did.

Finally, I set aside the fears of abandonment that kept me from accepting love and finding trust. I had decided to trust Maj with my story, and he had told me that he loved me. I carried my decision and his words with me, and he had remained a friend, just as he had promised. I had come to see that my friends could become family, that the exclusion that had so tortured me did not have to continue. I didn't have to remain tight in the bud. I could blossom.

Sitting in the dim lighting of my loft, I looked out the window at the ripples of water reflecting the moonlight shining from the starry sky and wrote to him, "Thank you for teaching me. I feel accepted. I trust you and I believe you when you say that you love me."

Before drifting to sleep that night, I received his reply, "Your teacher comes when you are ready and not before. Most of the teaching has little to do with words. You feel like a receiver of the invisible tidings, a receiver moving toward becoming a creator. I have no doubt you see me for who I am. There is a great consolation and possibility in that. All relationships of the soul leave us on the brink of the Nameless. I feel as if I have much to give you now. Many miles between us. But it all will find you. Much of it already has. Remember: 'Attentiveness is the natural prayer of the soul.' The transmission this day is at a deep level. Is anything different with you, some opening? Loving, Maj."

Back in R's office, my trustworthy therapist tried to convince me to quit trying to get my parents and sister to understand my suffering. He said that I was still rigid, tense, and guarded, but that I was getting better. I tried to explain how hard it was to eat, to smile, to talk to people. "Accept God's love," he said to me. He'd always had a way of stating simple remedies just when I felt things couldn't get any more complicated.

"Are you seriously pointing me to the cross right now?" I asked in frustration.

"No, I'm asking you to take yourself off of it," he admonished.

It was as if the rest of the world stopped moving as this forced epiphany joined my faith in a lucid moment that I would continue to struggle against but never be able to deny. I was never supposed to be the sacrificial lamb.

Chapter Eleven

"Abstain from every form of evil."
(I Thessalonians 5:22)

Spirit Lake bustled with the anticipation of another summer. The air was filled with aroma from the Belladonna lilies that surrounded *Our Lady of Guadalupe* in the yard of the cabin. Maj told me that these flowers come into their full glory in late summer and are referred to as "naked ladies." Continuing to coax me from the rigid, tense, and guarded shell that R had also identified, he expanded the possibilities for blossoming. I could be one of the yellow tulips that lined the east wall of the cabin. I could be the cheerful, star-like blossom of a Grecian windflower. Perhaps my scent was the honeysuckle that ran along the west edge of the dam of our favorite lake. Bradley built a cart to shuttle Maj from the front porch of the cabin to the fishing boat. Wood, nails, and wheels came together to form a vehicle for our paragon. We called it *One Trick Pony*, painting its name in red letters beneath an image of a foal with a long, disheveled mane waving behind him. I was looking forward to another summer of memories and love, but one thing was markedly different. My sweet neighbor was confined to the nursing home, and she wouldn't be returning. My heart ached for her, and I committed to include her in whatever way I could and began thinking about traveling to visit her in her distress. As the days passed--the end of each one bringing us closer to the relaxed, blissful feeling of getaway that summer provided--Maj sent uplifting words, spiritual reflections, philosophical ruminations, and snippets of thoughts to ponder. I opened my email to one such thought, derived from a Delphic oracle. He said to let these words live in my journal:

The lines are cast; the nets are set and waiting. Now, the tunnies come, slipping through the moonlit sea.

"Have you ever felt that you were faced with pure evil?" R asked me during a long conversation about my troubles. Resistant, my eyes wandered around the room as my mind searched for a matter less menacing to my psyche. Not willing to enable my denial, he posed a second question, "How about when you were being raped?" I responded to him with pained eyes that were thankful that he understood. That knowledge of good and evil had plagued me as I searched for the truth available among many masquerading lies, but I had never been able to name it, let alone, have someone speak it truthfully to me so that my ears could hear the words. It was vital, he said, to identify both the truth and the lie in any situation. Weeks later, facing another bout of psychogenic urinary retention on the afternoon of a day that I had therapy, he called me to offer advice to get me through the hours leading up to my appointment. "Go to the bathroom and release your anger. You can do it," he told me. "The truth is that it is waste, and you can let it go. The lie is that you have to keep it." I had never expected such profound psychological insight to come from physical symptoms. It was the first time I understood the depth of the connection between mind and body.

As if Maj truly was the sorcerer his name implied, he sent me a letter speaking to the awareness I had so recently acquired. "You have a soul issue, Talia. Can you work on the soul through the body? Yes. But you need someone who knows the way, who has the map. You have the bravery to act on this. I am here. I love you. I accept you. You have medical issues that are outside R's ken. Think hard about this. Loving, Maj."

I was struck by the timing of the shared understanding of my condition from my two surrogate fathers, but I did not know what to make of his disparaging remark about R. I didn't agree, and I didn't want R to be offended. I decided I would protect my protector from the comment, so I never told him.

With summer approaching, I strove to do the things that I believed should come easier to me. Go to work. Be a mother. Be a wife. Standing in the bathroom, baggy clothes hanging from my slight frame, I asked my husband to be the mirror for me. "Do I look sick?"

Vexed and unable to help, he replied, "You don't get to ask me if you look sick. You are sick, and I know you are sick."

He was right, and I felt like a failure. Days later a co-worker saw a cut on my arm and called me crazy. I fled my office and found myself in the dark corner of the nearest hallway, where I tried not to fulfill her prophecy. Overwhelmed by the feedback I was receiving, I called R in tears, afraid I was losing my mind. With the certainty I needed, he told me that I was not out of touch with reality, and he stayed with me on the phone until my anxiety subsided. I was relieved I wasn't going insane, but I felt that he was the only reason I wasn't.

Maj and his wife made the five-hundred-mile journey to the cabin without his mom. I drove up the road one day, and there he was. He held up his hand and waved at me through the window. I mirrored the gesture, and when I got out of my car he said, "The open-handed wave is how we let each other know that we are unarmed." The neighborhood picked up where it had left off, as the guys baited their lines, piled into an old canoe, and listened to the scratchy songs of the bold red-winged blackbirds soaring through the air. I put on my gold one-piece swimming suit and explored my Silkie side as I swam to the dam and back. Feasts of salmon patties and roasted vegetables were eaten at picnic tables while we planned dessert for the following day. I baked blackberry cobblers that Maj couldn't stop eating and tracked down gooseberries from my grandmother so that Maj's wife could make a pie. Though troubled and sick, I enjoyed witnessing the happiness of others. I settled in for the warmth of summer.

That warmth never came. One morning in June as I was sitting at my office desk, feigning the role of functional employee, I heard the familiar ding of an email notification. My countenance lifted when I saw that it was from R. Then, the rug was pulled out from under me and my heart shattered. The black and white letters on the computer screen drained me of hope.

"I regret to inform you that due to personal circumstances, I have made the decision to retire. Effective immediately."

The remainder of the message faded away as tears blurred my vision and spilled onto my face. I stood and ran away from the message, and my job. Sitting in my car at the city park, I read his email over and over.

"I sincerely apologize for what this will cause in you," he wrote. "If you would like to continue therapy via text and email, I would be happy and willing to do that."

He'd thrown me a life preserver. He also included the name of a colleague he felt confident to recommend should I choose not to continue communicating with him. I knew I would accept his offer to treat me over the phone, but I was grief stricken. I had thought I would see him the following day, but now I would never see him

again. I worried that something bad had happened to him, to his
wife, or family. I wondered if he was sick. I knew that I would never
find out what had happened to cause such a sudden departure, so I
prayed for him. He had told me once that his words would go with
me, that I would take him out into the world with me even after I
learned to walk on my own. It was his last words at my first
appointment that played in my mind on repeat, a soundtrack that
further saddened a mind too devastated to contemplate anger: *You
are not helpless or hopeless, and I will not abandon you.*

    I was crushed. I replied to his email and told him I would like
to continue communicating with him but added that I didn't know if
it was fair to him. I had no idea what was going on in his life and did
not want to burden him. I asked how payment would take place
under these circumstances.

    I thought back to a morning when I had texted him with my
stress and trepidation before eight o'clock in the morning. He wrote
back, "I'm already in the office. Come here." I walked into the office
and found him, his pipe hanging from his mouth, sorting through
papers at his desk. "Good morning!" he greeted me as his hands
motioned to the womb chair. He helped me work through my
concerns until I had to go to work.

    As I stood to leave, I reached for my pocketbook saying, "I
need to pay you."

    He lowered his chin and raised his eyebrows as he deflected
my insult and said, "I'm not a lawyer. Go to work."

    By the time I'd reflected on this memory, his response came
through, "I'm not going to take anything from you. I care about what
happens to you."

    I was dejected, yet grateful.

    I went home to the lake, but my globe was breaking, spider
cracks spreading through the glass, threatening to let in the peril it
was supposed to shield. When I looked up at the sun shining from
the blue sky, I saw, instead, the dark grey of ominous thunderclouds
bringing a storm. I plodded into the house and collapsed onto the
dark brown sectional, burying my head into a red throw pillow,
inconsolable. Hours later, I still had not turned from my mourning.
The house phone rang. I picked it up, wiping tears from my face
before answering.

"Talia?"

It was Maj, calling from next door.

"The first gooseberry pie just came out of the oven. I wanted to invite you over to eat with us."

I could barely pull myself from my misery enough to form words, let alone think about food. "My shrink retired," I said flatly.

There was a long silence on the other end of the line as I started to cry.

"Do you feel abandoned?" Maj asked.

Of course! I thought. But not wanting to accuse R of such a thing, I shrugged my shoulders, as if Maj could see my response through the walls of each of our homes. He continued to wait for an answer, but I never spoke.

"Let's do this," he said. "I'll save you a piece of pie, and you and I can talk a little later. We've got a house full over here, and I understand why you aren't up to that right now."

I agreed and hung up the phone. I wondered what I would have done had Maj not been next door when this tragedy struck. I knew he would support me through this loss. My husband and son went about their normal activities around me, but I was frozen in grief. I had lost my shield, and though I had known he was playing a crucial role in my life, I had no idea how much I would still need his protection.

I didn't think anyone could help me, but I hoped Maj could. I knew he would try. The next day, I followed a broken concrete path overgrown with grass and dandelions down to the dock. Maj was lying on his belly, facing towards me as I approached, his withered legs pointing down the long pier toward Spirit Lake. The water sparkled like crystals behind him, the vast, azure sky was cloudless, and the sun warmed my skin and reflected the golden tints hidden in my dark hair. Conditions were perfect for the patient fisherman before me.

I took my place in front of him, sitting Indian style with my long, braided hair covering half of my sulking face. Our neighbors and spouses were talking and laughing nearby, carrying rafts down to the water and preparing to enjoy the tropical atmosphere of our little cove. But I stayed with the only person who knew my secrets and was willing to talk to me about them face to face.

Tentatively, he broke the silence and began, "You know, Talia, I really want to be truthful with you. Is that ok?"

I nodded my head yes, looking for words of comfort from my trusted counselor, a man who had helped me learn how to be mindful of the present moment, who taught me to breathe colors, feel the wind, and believe in the strength of the flower that could bloom even during the harshest winters.

"I'm having trouble not being one of the men who wants you," he said. He gazed at me, hypnotically, his eyes unfaltering. I was bewildered, unable to fathom what he was trying to tell me. But then he made himself clear. "I want to fuck you once and come in you six times."

Suddenly, I was floating above the pier, above the water. My eyes remained fixed, but I could no longer feel the planks of the wooden dock beneath me. I was watching us from the outside. His stare was unrelenting, I found myself in a trance. For a moment, I wondered who he was. But then, his familiar voice reached for me again.

"I'm not like the men who have abused you," he said, shaking his head and adding, "I want no part of that."

I dropped my head and stared at the cracks between the grey, weathered boards. My mind was searching for something to hold onto. Silent, I couldn't think of any words to say, until his voice broke the stillness, and I looked at him again.

"Do you want me to drift away like a cloud then?" he asked.

I looked away, into the mossy lake water lapping onto the shore. I felt like I was bleeding, like it would be no surprise to find blood dripping from my nose or pouring from my body. The question dumbfounded me. How could he threaten to drift away when he knew I was in absolute anguish over R's retirement? Minutes passed before he spoke to me again.

"I thought long and hard about whether you could handle this. You are a strong, blooming flower. I knew you could carry this, that you would welcome my honesty."

I wanted to be strong. I didn't want to be deserted, again. And that's how he caught me. The words that had come from his mouth had frightened me, but faced with the possibility of him disappearing, I decided that I could handle the words. After all, they were only *words*. I certainly didn't feel I had the right to reprimand a man well over twice my age. He had accepted everything that I had told him about myself without judgment. What kind of a person was I if I couldn't handle his honesty, like he believed I could? Still, I glanced around at the people, close friends, our spouses even, who were only yards away. What was I going to do, tell on him? Since I'd first met him years ago, he had done nothing but speak encouragement and bear my burdens with me. How could I run to others with what he had said when he had held my secrets when nobody else would? I would show him that I could carry it. I wouldn't tell anyone. Time would pass, his words would fade into the past and I would not mention them again. I would remain a friend.

As I was thinking this, our neighbors joined us. Maj resumed his role of deep-thinking, poetic elder. I smiled and began acting. Acting like I was fine. Acting like I hadn't seen and felt evil. And, I pulled it off. Everyone saw what I appeared to be. Nobody knew who I was.

My new family couldn't tell that everything had changed, and I decided to keep it that way. I was not willing to be at the center of another family dissolution, especially over only a few words. Besides, Maj would never hurt me. As people came and went throughout the afternoon, I found myself alone with him again. Apologetically, he said, "Talia, ignore that drift away stuff. I don't know why I said it. I won't abandon you. I don't know how."

There was that word again. My nemesis. R may have had to leave, but Maj was still here. I managed a half-smile before I stood to go get changed for dinner. My husband was grilling steaks and potatoes for the whole clan. My orange sarong didn't seem to be functioning as a cover-up anymore, as I walked self-consciously back to my house. I looked up at the sky, at the ceiling of my globe, the cracks had shattered into shards of glass that hung precariously over me in a darkening paradise.

Chapter Twelve

"For of this sort are those who creep into households and make
captives of gullible women loaded down with sins, led away by
various lusts."
(II Timothy 3:6)

In the shower before dinner, I tried to resolve my conflicting emotions. I felt bad, but I didn't think I had done anything wrong. I felt guilty for not telling my husband what Maj had said. My mind wandered back to another time that I had felt anxious after talking to Maj.

A couple of weeks earlier, I had sat on the cool concrete of the cabin's front porch until nearly midnight. Candles were flickering, the hot wax dripping down the sides and forming pools on the ground. I could hear the deep, restful breathing of Maj's wife on the other side of the screened windows where she lay sleeping. I had been telling Maj about my relationship with my father, expressing remorse over my drug problems, and relaying the guilt I had about not being a better wife to my husband. "Father issues are particularly thorny," he told me. In regard to the drugs, he said with a grin, "So, you got high. Forgive yourself." It was late, and as I stood to leave, he opened his arms for a hug. I lowered myself to my knees in front of him and accepted his embrace. He pulled me close and then released my body, only to pull me into himself again. He repeated this in a slow, rocking motion, and it went on for longer than was comfortable. I told him goodnight and walked the few steps to my own front door.

As I entered my home, I encountered my husband walking through the dining room. Feeling unsettled, I stopped him and reported, "Maj just gave me a hug goodnight." He looked at me as if he were waiting for me to tell him something else, something that mattered. "It didn't feel right. Something was off," I said.

"Maj hugs everybody," he replied nonchalantly.

I tried to be more direct. "I feel bad about it."

"He's a 72-year-old man in a wheelchair," he said with a grin. "He doesn't think of you like that."

I was embarrassed for having thought something was wrong. I was even more embarrassed for having said it.

After dinner, we sat by the water's edge and watched the

blazing, orange sun hover over the earthen dam before disappearing into a grove of hickory, ash, oak, and maple. My head was still spinning from the conversation that had forced some part of me to retreat from my body and hover above us on the dock. Each time I try to recall the memory of him professing sexual feelings toward me, it feels like a dream, like I can't find all the pieces of the memory. I try to imagine myself sitting there before him, but I can never ground myself to the dock. I had not stayed there. It was as if my mind had left the borders of my arms, legs, head, and chest, my consciousness transcending my physical form. What is more strange is that it was a familiar feeling.

It was a long time before I realized that the sense of *Deja vu* that I had felt in those moments stemmed from the evening when R had pulled me out of a panic attack and down from the space where I had been drifting above our chairs. I began wondering what R would say about what had taken place. I was sure that I would tell him in person at an appointment, if I still had one, but I couldn't conceive of typing out the words that Maj had spoken to me and sending them in an impersonal text message.

Clairvoyantly, Maj began questioning me. "How are you handling the retirement?"

I felt a knot forming in my throat as I tried, unconvincingly, to be brave. "He has to do what's best for him. He didn't really leave me. I'm allowed to write to him."

Maj pursed his lips and looked at me as if he felt sorry for me. "He's gone, Talia. He's not really here. Can you see him? Can you hear his voice? I think what he's doing is harmful to you, stringing you along while he lengthens your pain. I don't want you to hurt."

I held back the fountain of tears. A fountain that I carried with me, releasing only a little at a time, for months and years to come.

As day turned to night, Maj assured me that I was going to be okay. He reminded me that I had already done incredible work, sloughing off the old layers in preparation for this moment. His calm voice and ingratiating presence made me feel secure as he persuaded me that I would shine on past this difficult phase.

"You're a brave heart, Rosebud. We'll get through this."

I thought of the cliché phrase I had heard as a child: *Bloom where you are planted*. I knew I needed to accept my circumstances and the opportunities for growth that were available and to be grateful for the present situation. Suddenly, Maj's voice broke through the silence of the night.

"Do you get wet?" he asked.

My mind took longer than usual to process such a frank question. I felt completely exposed, like when my sweatpants had been jerked off my body. It was a yes or no question, but the answer was stuck in my throat. It occurred to me that he already knew the answer. After all, I was an adult woman in her twenties, and while naive to conversations of this level of openness, I was not absent of libido. I felt like I had to fill the awkward silence, so I answered.

"Well, yeah."

He smiled. "Good. I'm hard right now."

Looking back, I can see how Maj had slowly indoctrinated me. It started with a shared interest, spirituality. I can't count the number of times that I studied or journaled about something, only for Maj to mention the exact concept the next time I spoke to him. Very soon after I met him, I was writing about the importance of renewing your mind daily, a concept I had learned from Paul's Epistle to the Romans. The very next day, I went to visit Maj's mother. She, too, reads The Good Book, so it was not unusual for me to acknowledge my faith in God to her. I did so that day, saying that while life was hard and unpredictable, I knew God had a plan for my life. Maj's ears seemed to perk up and he complimented my curiosity in the plan, calling me a searcher. Maj often referenced God, and it was clear to anyone that met him that he was a deep, spiritual thinker.

Shortly after I mentioned my faith, Maj scooted across the living room floor of the cabin and positioned himself on the carpet between his mother and me. He began sharing his wisdom and used a phrase I had never heard, *tikkun olam*. He explained that it was a Hebrew phrase that referred to the daily repair of one's world. This was the first of many synchronicities that I experienced with him. Wanting to share the serendipity, I opened my journal to the page where I had just journaled about the same notion of daily renewal that brings forth transformation. He was excited by the shared learning and called it *transmission*. This type of coincidence happened throughout my work with R. Maj would often begin teaching me about something just as R was helping me with it, without my ever mentioning the topic. It just seemed to happen, supernaturally. The connection was undeniable, and the advice from the two was always similar.

Maj's instruction didn't begin to change in a way that I could see until R was further away from me and I was grieving his absence in my life. My grief definitely affected my decision making, but I had not yet realized that my ability to make choices was already prone to error due to the abuse I had already suffered and the extended period of time I had spent in my family, unable to receive help and continually in the presence of the man who had hurt me. For an entire year, I did many things that I didn't want to do. I did many things that I didn't want anyone to know about. Though I regret many of those choices, I have learned that if I didn't want anyone to know about them, I shouldn't have done them in the first place. The same is true for every person who finds himself in this story.

After opening up about my sexual assaults to Maj, he showed sympathy and talked about compassion and empathy, but he did not focus on the abuse that had occurred. He came alongside me, and we grew much closer, but he never really talked about what had happened to me. It seemed that he simply accepted it with me, and that was good enough. It was more than most had offered. I didn't realize until much later that what I was seeing in his lack of reaction to my stories was a disregard for the seriousness of my experiences. After R retired, though, he became interested in talking openly to me about my sexual healing. Asking me about my own sexual arousal before admitting his was the beginning of a teaching about shame.

Psychologist Carl Jung called shame a soul eating emotion, and I was being eaten alive. Maj could see this and knew that I carried much shame in regard to my sexual abuse. He told me that it shouldn't be so. That was true. I should not have had to feel shame about decisions that I didn't even make, about acts that had been forced upon me. Maj did a good job of representing the fact that those harmful things that had happened years before did not need to rob me of my own sexual expression, in the present. I wanted to be relieved of my shame, and he postulated that my achieving this would help my marriage. Though his question about me "getting wet" seemed inappropriate to me, he spent a considerable amount of time praising my ability to accept my own impulses as good and to reject the way the past had been controlling me. I thought it was perhaps immaturity on my part that made me feel uncomfortable in our conversations, a thought that was reinforced by the age difference between us and his sporadic references to me being an adult.

The truth is that my development was an absolute mess, interrupted and delayed by abuse and subsequent addiction. I had made progress through psychotherapy with R and knew that simply talking could be extremely beneficial. Even after Maj said such foul things to me, I told myself that talking to him could still be useful. I did, however, try to protect myself from Maj's vulgar attack on the dock, but the defense that I used was denial. I felt like I was being faced with evil, so I told myself that they were only words. I held onto the belief that he would never hurt me. Being dominated or exploited again was simply not going to happen. I would not allow it. Nobody would ever force me onto my back again. My wrists would never again be pinned above my head. It turns out, they wouldn't have to be, and lucky for Maj, since he lacked the physical ability to dominate me. Nonetheless, that didn't mean that he couldn't corner and control me. I had noticed the first time I met him that his intellectual capacity overshadowed his physical limitation. With his body stricken with polio, his mind ascended to higher mastery. He was not physically able to obtain all that he wanted, so learned ways to solve that problem with suggestions of the imagination wrapped in beautiful words. A mutation occurred, and he discovered how to manipulate the world as he whispered incantations in the ears of the people around him. Maj is smart. He was smarter than me. He would never have to hold me down or bind my wrists. Instead, he would rape my mind first. My body would be used later.

The day after Maj began his teaching on shame, I was tanning myself on the dock. The green and yellow fabric of my one-piece suit was covered with a pattern of umbrellas and foliage. I lay on the pier, a towel around my waist, as I soaked up the early afternoon sun. Maj was to my left, and Bradley to my right. They talked over me, as they discussed fishing plans for that evening. As Bradley stood and walked slowly up the driveway to his home, Maj saw an opportunity for further instruction.

"Talia, I want you to do something for me. Reach underneath that towel, touch yourself with your fingers and offer them to me."

My heart began to race, I looked over my shoulder and around the cove for signs of other people. I wished Bradley had not left.

"Go on, I'll look away," he prodded.

My heart was racing.

"Do it," he said.

I closed my eyes for a moment before I reached down, between my legs, and touched myself. Maj didn't continue looking away like he'd said he would. As I brought my hand out from beneath the colorful, terrycloth, towel, he grabbed my hand suddenly and forced my fingers into his mouth. I looked away, humiliated.

Later that night, he sent me a two-sentence email: "Last bite of the gooseberry. First taste of the peach."

It's not easy to explain how it happens, how the word *no* can be deleted from a person's vocabulary. I think it starts the first time saying no doesn't work. When the most sacred part of yourself is violated, your will is defied. When control belongs to another person and not yourself, your agency crumbles. It continues as you realize that neither your inner-self nor your outer-self was able to protect you from danger.

Had I ever said the word *no* before? Yes, of course I did. But what had I gained from my resistance? This is why I had accepted Maj's nurturing friendship in the first place. I wanted to be understood, and Maj listened, but he did not allow me to dwell in the past. His continual teaching was to live in the present moment, to "kiss the joy as it flies." Over the course of several years, I had developed admiration for a man who had overcome his own burdens with joy and purpose. I had thought that he wanted to help me. I hoped that he could. I believed he would.

Maj had promised that he would tell me only the truth. He had said that he loved me, and I wanted to believe that I could be loved. Then he said that he wanted to use my body, and I had wanted to believe that he could be trusted not to violate that trust. I was still haunted by the fallout of my previous traumas, the way I had lost everyone close to me when I had not been believed. I had lost my family. I had lost R. What now could I do? I did not want Maj to float away, too.

I had invested much time into seeking out protection and care. I was sure that I had found it, in R, and then in Maj. But I had lost R, and Maj's face had now split in two. In my stress, I returned to what I knew, which was to remain silent and to protect the reputation of a man who had exposed a dark side to me. I knew how to do that. Over the next several months, I would continually downplay in my mind the implications of my inability to tell him no on the dock that day. He had crossed a line. He had used more than words when he grabbed my wrist with his hand and forced my fingers into his mouth, but I minimized that as well. I told myself that if I had known what was going to happen, I would not have complied. I would have said no.

The truth, though, is that he had overpowered me -- even though it didn't happen all at once as it had in the hotel room. Instead, he had taken years to prepare me for that moment. It wasn't even that difficult for him to groom me since much of the work had been done for him before he even met me. I had already been weakened from previous battles, and I was tired of fighting. I wasn't even willing to admit that I had found myself in the arena again. So, I held onto an illusion of control so that I would not feel helpless. If he ever asked me to do something bad again, I comforted myself to believe that I could say no.

But I was lying to myself. Not one time would I ever manage to tell Maj Ragain no. Instead, I made a trade. A compromise. You can hurt me. Just don't leave me.

Chapter Thirteen

"And I, where could I take my shame?"
(II Samuel 13:13)

My shame grew like a spreading infection, and it followed me everywhere, contaminating every environment and keeping me from believing that I had true value. I had hoped that I could recover within the safety of my new lakeside paradise. However, after R retired, Maj was the only one left who offered me any hope that I could get better, and he offered a way for me to be unashamed. Instead, the cycle began again: secrecy, silence, and judgment. I had been given a new secret by a new man that I could not share with anyone, and Maj continually reinforced my silence, telling me that we could not tell others what we were doing because the others were simple, heartless people who lacked the courage to understand the path he had chosen for me to walk with him.

"All around me I see people acting out of fear and denial, living in one little room of a sun struck mansion," he told me.

Eventually, he said that the erotic path and the spiritual path were the same path. Over much time, he led me down the dark road with him, and I found myself treading a path of fire. I withheld the judgment of others by hiding the truth about my relationship with Maj, but I judged myself because I knew that it was wrong.

Also, I felt guilty for the unforgiveness I held toward others in regard to my past abuse. He played upon my inadequate but well-intentioned faith and desire to be spiritually taught. One day he said to me, "You're forgiving me even as I do this, aren't you? That's incredible. You are amazing." I didn't want to judge him. I ended up finding myself in a trap. I hadn't realized the lines were cast long ago, that the nets were set and waiting. I wouldn't have stepped into the trap purposefully, but once I found myself in it, I didn't know how to escape. I had looked for a new family because I wanted the opportunity for things to turn out differently, not to be abandoned by a father, not to be abused by a brother, not to lose my entire family in the process. Maj had ensnared me with the empathetic nature he displayed to everyone he met, but what I first recognized as empathy turned out to be a shiny lure. It was good bait, and he caught me, long before I learned that Spirit Lake was treacherous water that hid a lurking sea dragon.

From the beginning, Maj reconstructed our encounters and fed them back to me. Of the exchange on the dock where he told me he wanted to fuck me and come in me; he wrote:

> *Your eyes. That moment on the pier was extraordinary.*
> *Those colored tides that wash around inside you, that tug at*
> *me, the river that I am, had risen to eye level in you. It was as*
> *if I was seeing inside you, and I knew you wanted me to do*
> *that, that you were opening to me, showing me the deep*
> *colors of your one wild and precious life. Then, the clouds*
> *moved across that inner sky, not cool but heated, and pulling*
> *at me. That is exactly what I saw in that moment. Then the*
> *wet. Then my burning bowl. The kind of moment the gods*
> *brood over. I miss you. Tell me your dreams.*

This is what had happened, he was telling me, but I had not remembered it the same way. It was true that on that day, my eyes had held trust for him, but when he spoke aloud his lustful thoughts, I was struggling to reconcile the upheaval. He spoke now of my opening to him, an opening I did not remember. He spoke of my wild and precious life, a life I felt was frightened and tortured. He spoke of my wetness and the burning bowl between his legs. I remember a wise, caring man who till that moment had made me feel that it was possible to be safe.

It had all started with him asking permission to be honest with me. In my effort to keep him on the pedestal I had allowed him to ascend in my heart, I began to wonder if perhaps it was keeping his dark side hidden that would have been scarier for me. Maybe exposing it truly was an act of honesty, of kindness. He had been telling me for such a long time that only the truth was kind. In the days following his announcement on the pier, I walked around in a daze of disillusionment, like when you are on your way to a funeral but the sun is shining, the birds are chirping, and the blue skies seem to show no acknowledgment of the loss that has occurred. As it turned out, I would soon be on my way to a funeral.

In the midst of confusion, as I was trying to make sense of it all, my grandfather died. I contacted R to check in, tell him about the loss of my grandpa and ask for some help. I couldn't talk to him as much as I wanted, perhaps less than I needed, but I was grateful to be able to speak to him at all. I still couldn't imagine texting the words that Maj had spoken, so I fumbled along in a texting conversation, trying to express that things with Maj had gotten complicated. R asked if it would be easier for me to explain things to him if he called me. I said that it would, and he called my phone, just a short time before I needed to leave for the graveside service.

I told him Maj's confession, verbatim.

"Damnit, Damnit, Damnit!" R yelled into the phone. "Why did he have to do this?!"

My eyes grew wide as I heard the man I knew to be gentle and calm raise his voice in anger.

"That is completely inappropriate. What he's doing is wrong!"

It felt good to tell someone the truth, and to receive an appropriate response. I could tell he wanted me to be protected. We agreed to talk more later because I had to leave for my grandfather's service. Before R hung up the phone, he said, "Don't allow yourself to be left alone with him."

I arrived at the cemetery and joined my family, but I felt a growing sense of disconnection from them, a connection that had nearly been severed completely. I didn't feel that I belonged with them anymore. My paternal grandfather had died on my father's birthday, and my heart ached for my dad. Standing over the grey tombstone with my grandmother and grandfather's names on it, I texted my part-time shrink a question about why Maj had done what he did to me. I asked R, "What is this, preying on weakness?" As people began to filter slowly out of the graveyard his reply came through, "I'm sorry. Yes."

I knew R believed that my trust had been violated, but I was unwilling to give up on Maj. I still felt that he had shown me much good before things changed, and I did not know how to separate the bad from the good. I was determined to hold onto the good. Things could turn out differently this time, I told myself. I had always believed that he was capable of helping me, and he continued to preach that the help he had to offer would finally liberate me from the torments with which I had lived for many years.

He kept referring back to the moment on the dock when he asked me to touch myself as a reminder of what I had learned, but what I learned during this exchange was that I could not bring myself to say no to him. He told me I was growing stronger, but I felt I was growing weaker. Much later, I realized that my obedience to his command had been carefully cultivated by him for a very long time. It had begun with requests to read books that he suggested or to consider teachings he had collected over his long years of study. It spread to my taking care of his home, the cabin, where I began nesting rituals in preparation for weeks of his return. Later, he asked me to hang bird feeders, practice yoga, and of course, plant flowers. His request on the pier had been a tipping point. When it happened, I suddenly feared that I had lost control. Maybe I never had been in control, but I had not realized it until that moment.

After saying goodbye to my grandfather, my family gathered at my sister's house. Should I stay with my birth family and continue to keep their secrets while they mourned the loss of our grandfather, or should I return to the broken globe of my lakeside neighborhood and keep the secrets of my new family, a family that was still filled with laughter, love, and togetherness because its secret had not yet been exposed? Maj's son and granddaughters had arrived once again, deepening the family atmosphere that I longed to enjoy. I chose to be with them, with Maj's family that was becoming my own, and to live in happiness and denial instead of grief and shame.

At the cabin, I had joined Maj's family for dinner following my grandfather's funeral. As I pushed the food around my plate, R wrote to check on me and began talking to me about what I was experiencing:

> *You have unresolved issues from not having a positive father-daughter relationship. The subconscious is non-negotiable about childhood needs that must be met. People will look for those needs to be met in an adult that reminds you of a parent. You have been repeatedly hurt by men, and you need to deal with your anger. Start with Maj, it is fresh. You know the truth, but you don't want to believe it.*

I noticed that Maj was looking at me disapprovingly as I concentrated on my cell phone. He never liked it when people were lost in their devices instead of enjoying the present.

"Who are you talking to?" he asked.

"R," I answered.

Annoyed, he shook his head. "He's gone, Talia. You have to let go of that. Were you sleeping with him or something?"

Astonished, I immediately defended myself, "No! Absolutely not. Are you kidding me?"

He shrugged his shoulders and said dismissively, "I wouldn't know if that was part of your relationship with him or not."

I felt like I had just been accused of incest, and my offense was obvious. Did he really think I was capable of that? I told R goodbye and spent the rest of the night on the porch. I ignored my phone and tried to enjoy the present. Maj's charm returned, as it always did. I forced a smile as I feared what I knew was inevitable, that my relationship with R would end. After Maj had accused me of having sex with my shrink, I decided I'd have to let go of both of them. Everything was getting too complicated. I remembered R's analogy of a child learning to walk and thought that I should let go of the hand that I had once trusted and learn to walk alone.

Over the remainder of Maj's stay, I tried to focus on the people and the lake. We built a fire pit and roasted hot dogs and marshmallows by the water. I climbed into the kayak and paddled beneath weeping willow trees. I sat on the dock and talked to Greg about work, life, and loss. I called Maj's mother and included her as much as I could in the fellowship that she was missing, looking out the bay window of my living room and telling her what I saw. Maj's wife cutting his hair on the end of the pier. Her grandson swimming with his daughters into the middle of the lake. My son holding the hands of her great granddaughters as they walked down the road. I told her that my son was learning how to swim. I taught my son how to hold his breath and go under the water. I was teaching him to stay afloat, but I felt like I was drowning. I went days without eating, I was popping Xanax like candy, and my cutting got worse. Still, I was working out in my mind how when Maj left to go back home, I would let go of my dependency on him and settle my conscience. Having done that, I wouldn't need R quite as badly, and I would release him into his retirement. Maybe my husband would finally be able to understand what I'd been going through. I hoped that things would get better.

Chapter Fourteen

"Love does not delight in evil but rejoices in the truth."
(I Corinthians 13:6)

As I was preparing to step away from Maj and R, I had a run in with my father. I was leaving his house one afternoon, and he caught a glimpse of a cut on my wrist. Turning my hand over with his, he stared at the self-inflicted injury. I looked up at him, my eyes filled with shame and pain. "You make no sense," he said. Then he walked away.

Maj called me that day, and I told him what my dad had said. He seemed very sad and talked to me about the reasons for my self-punishment, the abuse. He was warm and caring, his voice soft as he traveled back to those memories with me.

"When you go to cut yourself, picture my big hand closing over yours. I can't breathe and watch you do that. You have an extraordinary life ahead of you with your great loving heart, your openness. I'm not trauma. I love you."

The comfort flooded me, and I wasn't sure that I could follow through with my plan to cut ties with him. I needed to do it quickly before I lost my nerve. A couple of days later, I composed an email about my dependency problems and the guilt I felt for taking out my abandonment issues on others. I sent the message separately, to Maj and to R, and I offered to let go of my relationship with each of them. It was one message meant for both of them, but neither accepted my offer.

Instead, Maj expanded on his teaching about the open life and living unashamed. He was sure that I could claim what I thought had been stolen or lost. He was trying to teach me the "hard lesson" of trading my shame for love, wherever it might find me, and embracing it at every opportunity.

"My little flower," he wrote. "If we -- you and I -- learn nothing else from this, we must learn to go where the mystery and beauty reveal themselves. Never, ever forget that."

Maj said that as I did this, I could share my new confidence with my husband. He assured me that the work I was doing would benefit those around me. He said he had been living this way for a long time and that even his wife knew how to include it. All nurturing began with inclusion and learning to include others was the key as I moved forward. He promised healing as I learned to include others in the beautiful mysteries of life. Begin with myself, and him, and then widen the circle into an ever-growing family of love and acceptance.

This was a powerful teaching for me. I had wanted to be included desperately because I felt I had been excluded from my own family. He offered me another path, another family, another way to be a part of a community that would love and accept me. In any case, I had already grown accustomed to including his family in my life because he had taught me to do this. He once told me to throw a penny off of a bridge that I crossed every week. It was a bridge that his father had helped build, and he asked me to speak his father's name aloud into the universe every time I dropped a coin into the river that ran beneath. It was important that his father be remembered. But more, that Maj be remembered.

Maj also suggested that once he was gone from this world, I should write his name on a scrap of paper and put it into a bottle. He wanted me to throw that bottle off of his father's bridge and send it down the river to a distant shore where someone would find it and read his name aloud. The most central theme of all of Maj's teaching was that choosing to remember what happens between ourselves and another was The Way. It was the way to pay respect to your dealings with people, whether good or bad. It was the way to heal yourself from hurt. It was the way to make your life matter. It was the way to cope with loss.

Once as I stood on the bridge holding a phone to my ear, the wind blowing through my hair, Maj said to me, "Talia, a hundred years from now, nobody will even know your name."

I was willing to remember the names that were important to him. They became important to me, too. I traveled to his younger brother's grave and left a bouquet of flowers for the son whose mother would never stop thinking of him and loving him. Another day, I left a mason jar holding a single yellow rose. Maj was teaching me the power of remembrance.

A short time after I had begun considering the significance of inclusion and remembrance, Maj's son sent a message thanking me for the generosity and hospitality that my husband and I had shown to him and his daughters while they were visiting. A kind, adventurous, good spirited man, Maj's son had an engaging personality and contagious smile. He was a father, a successful businessman, and an avid outdoorsman. It was impossible for me not to like him, an inclination I wouldn't have resisted anyway since he was Maj's own flesh and blood. I told him that the lake wasn't the same when the Ragains weren't there, thanking him for an evening when we rocked on the cabin's front porch swing, listening to the ghost stories told by our neighbors and friends.

Maj had been preaching sexual awakening to me, and I was beginning to respond. On the swing that night, I felt a chemical attraction to the man sitting next to me, the son of my spiritual teacher. I wouldn't have acted upon it, but I was aware of it. This was uncharted territory, and I told my husband about it. He said that he was not concerned by the attraction because he knew nothing had happened between us. As I talked to Maj's son, mentioning the swing, it became clear that I was not the only one who had felt something on that swing.

"I tried really hard to ignore it. I avoided you out of respect, not because I wanted to," he confessed. "Dad picked up on it too," he said. "He asked if we were rubbing knees."

I appreciated his honesty and let him know that I had also been honest with my husband about what I was feeling. We chatted a while longer, about food, music, and the lake, before saying goodnight.

Later, Maj was upset. "I heard you and my son had a long talk," he said curtly. "A late night, too." What followed was what Maj called a tortured exchange. I had nothing to hide, and I was simply trying to accept what Maj had been teaching me about living in the present moment and accepting the fullness of my blossoming spirit. Besides, nothing happened. We had just talked. Maj told me that I should not shy away from whatever excites my spirit, then added, "But this is my son."

I was confused. I had thought that I wasn't supposed to feel ashamed, and I didn't know how to navigate the complexities of the path on which Maj was leading me. I had even tried to be kind by telling the truth to my husband and including him. Maj wanted me to be a part of his family, to say his father's name and remember his deceased brother, but apparently, not his living son. He was so disturbed that I made a decision to end the problem.

"He is your son. I do not have to talk to him. You do not have to talk to me. I won't accuse you of abandoning me."

There was a long silence before he responded. "This is a

passage through a strange, dangerous place with no markers," Maj said with a sigh. Let's let it fade. I want to keep talking to you. I love you." So, we put that behind us, and I understood that he expected a portion of my devotion to belong to him alone.

I wondered what love meant. He had told me that he loved me after I revealed to him the secrets of my past, but that was before he had confessed to being one of the men who wanted me. Now I didn't completely understand the meaning of the word. He said that he loved me, but the words began to carry a different significance in our relationship. Many of the men in my life had used those words towards me. My father. My boyfriends. My sister's boyfriend. Ever since I had gone from a thirteen-year-old tomboy to a fourteen-year-old cheerleader, boys and men had complimented me, calling me the prettiest girl in the room, before insulting me by grabbing my butt or making a crude comment. Did Maj love me the way he loved me when I'd told him that men had abused me, or now that he had begun talking to me about sex, did he love me in a different way? I wondered how I had gotten this far in life without understanding love.

I asked R what was wrong with me. Nothing was making sense. Love, sex, marriage: I couldn't get a handle on any of it, but I was sure my past had something to do with it.

"Your abuse has shaped who you are to a certain extent," he said carefully. "Accepting that is difficult but necessary. You did not choose for men to treat you the way they treated you. You did not receive love or sex correctly. Evil is how love was defined. You will need to redefine it. That's difficult. You need to separate as much as possible from evil."

I felt a heavy weight descend on my chest. *Evil* is how I had defined *love*? I couldn't begin to imagine how to fix such a flaw in my mind and in my heart, but there was one love about which I was certain: my love for Abram. No matter how broken my heart felt, my love for him was whole. He was my nearly constant companion, and our love for each other grew daily. Everything he did was interesting to me. Every day was an adventure. I wanted so badly to be a healthier person for him, so I kept trying to work through my issues to clear the static in my head. One night as I was tucking him into his bed, pulling the blanket covered with foxes, bears, and porcupines up to chin, I said, "I love you so much, Abram, and God loves you even more than that."

The days passed, and the time neared for Maj to leave again. One evening after dinner, he dialed his mother's phone number and the whole group took turns talking to her on the phone as twilight turned to dusk. As the others passed the phone around, I pictured her sitting in the lonely hallway of a nursing home, overworked aides rushing past her, a wheelchair under her broken hip. I spoke with her the longest, filling in the details of the trip she had missed, trying to give her a mental image that would make her happy, though I knew she had felt left out. After I hung up the phone, Maj suggested that it would brighten his mother's world for me to travel to visit her. I knew that it would, and I told him that I had considered it but wasn't sure that I felt safe traveling five hundred miles by myself. In the meantime, I would send inspirational cards and pictures of our family at the lake to remind her that I was holding her close. The conversation drifted, but my thoughts of his mother didn't. I had met her before I had met any of them. I had loved her first, and I was thankful to her, above all, that I had become a member of her family. When we said goodbye that evening, she had said, "I'm so glad I know you. Better late than never. I love you." I didn't want to miss whatever opportunities were left to spend time with her. I hoped that if I were meant to see her again, a way would appear.

As always, I was sad to see Maj go. The shift in his behavior had been a startling adjustment to make. Acknowledging my abandonment fears and offering to walk alone felt like a big step for me, but I felt relieved that both R and Maj had declined that offer. I had more trouble than I'd expected after Maj left. My destructive habits were catching up with me. I went days without eating, acting as if water, DXM, Xanax, and sunlight were going to get me through the day. Finally, I messaged R and told him how badly I was doing. I'd spent the whole day on the lake, trying to find some happiness, floating on a neon green raft, music playing from my laptop on the dock as I waited for a reply to my message to appear.

Eventually, R's response to my current state came through. "How can I help you if you go days without eating and don't tell me? I think you need more help than I am giving you."

My heart dropped, but I'd known this moment was coming, and I was tired of fearing and resisting it.

"I know. I understand," I replied, remorsefully.

After a few more exchanges, he wrote, "Thank you for trusting me."

I thanked him for being trustworthy as I tearfully accepted that my long relationship with my faithful counselor had come to an end.

"Follow the path God has for your life," he wrote. And with that, goodbye.

I had never experienced a goodbye more painful. As if my computer had conspired against me to make the moment as heart-wrenching as possible, the lyrics of a song played softly through the speakers. *Only know you love her if you let her go.* I knew R had gone because he wanted what was best for me, and he suggested I begin weekly therapy, as soon as possible, with the colleague he had mentioned before, a clinical psychologist just across the hall from R's old office. Being offered another therapist took none of the sting away, and I wasn't ready to walk by my old sanctuary and invite a new man into my mind.

I emailed the old man and told him it was over with R. Maj stepped up with renewed purpose.

Chapter Fifteen

"You shall not listen to the words of that prophet or that dreamer of dreams, for the Lord your God is testing you to know whether you love the Lord your God with all your heart and with all your soul."
(Deuteronomy 13:3)

Ending therapy took a toll on me. I knew that for many years I had turned to alcohol to cope when I could not turn to my family, and now that R was gone, too, my old habits grew worse, even though they were destroying me. Maj offered himself as an alternative, reminding me, "When we stop turning to people, we start turning to things, Talia." He imparted hope, saying that despite all that I had been through, something in me had protected the part of me that believed in love and the importance of finding a connection with others. He saw this in my love for my husband, my son, and in the way I had accepted his family. "It is all love's body. There's no way to separate love from anything else. Thankfully, you do not separate the parts. Almost everyone does, but not you."

Now that he had returned to his home, five-hundred miles away, the consternation I had felt about our encounters on the dock began to subside. My five-year wedding anniversary with my husband had just passed, and Maj said that the stability of my marriage was good for me, that I needed it and should be sure to take care of my husband. When I talked to Maj, I told him about my little family's escapades on the lake. We took our first voyage on a used boat that we had bought, and we taught Abram to ride a tricycle and fish. Maj said he taught his son to fish by tying a bread ball to a fishing line that he then hung from his boy's big toe. I imagined trying the same trick with Abram, but I couldn't imagine him standing still long enough to tie the knot.

Maj affectionately called my little boy Boogaloo, who was growing into a toddler. Like many young boys, he was developing a fascination with tractors. One day, I found an old coffee mug buried in the mud near Maj's dock. When I told him of my discovery he said, "It must be a John Deere mug, right? Give it to Boogaloo. He can drink his milk out of it." I appreciated the gift, but then he said something that was more precious to me than any well-wrapped package. "I love your son. You know that, don't you?" It seemed silly to keep worrying about losing another family. Maj cared about all of us. Our families had been blessed to end up next door to each other, where we could live and grow and love together. I thought of his mother, confined to the nursing home, and how much I loved and missed her. How extraordinary that I would develop such a close friendship with a woman, so late in her life, who would exemplify for me a mother's love, loss, and perseverance. It was an unexpected pleasure, us meeting each other and finding much in common, despite our generational differences. Maj admired the relationship between his mother and me. "In every house, make a place for crazy love," he told me. "Never turn away from crazy love, all your life."

Soon, my opportunity to visit the motherly neighbor I had been calling on the phone, sending cards, and praying for seemed to appear out of thin air. Greg, a lakeside neighbor and life-long friend of Maj's with whom I had grown very close, sent me a message one evening.

"Sis, you ready to make the trip to the nursing home?"

I was elated, but surprised. "How?" I asked.

"I have Columbus Day off. I'll drive us there that weekend. We can stay at Maj's. Bradley wants to come, too."

I smiled at the way things were coming together. I had spent the summer trying to include her in the life at the lake that she was missing, the life to which I anchored her, as Maj had said. But I hadn't felt that cards and phone calls had done enough. I knew that a true friend would visit the widow in her distress, and I felt that God had made a way for that. I yelled across the house to my husband and told him about the road trip that was being planned. He knew how badly I wanted to see her and that it was the long drive alone that had prevented me from going. He told me to go and to have a good time and that he would take care of Abram while I was away. I wrote back to Greg. "Thanks! I can't wait!"

My upcoming visit with Maj's mother gave me a kind of hope, a beacon that penetrated the fog to which I had grown accustomed. During the weeks leading up to our excursion, our excitement mounted. Greg, Bradley, and I anticipated bringing some joy to our friend in the nursing home, taking time off from our jobs, and travelling to visit the family that made the long drive to our neck of the woods each summer. Maj called me often to check the status of our plans, and I settled back into the friendship that had taken years to develop, the relationship that offered me hope, the bond I was afraid to lose. I knew that every relationship took twists and turns on the road to discovery, and Maj had said that adventure was the best way to learn.

As I spoke to him on the phone one afternoon, he spoke about the connections that had formed over the past several years as a larger family had mystically formed from friendships based on love and trust, housed safely by the enchanted Lake of Spirit that brought us all together. "There's no turning back now, Talia. We've crossed the boundaries into family. This is forever." I thought of his mother's age and declining health. I knew that one day I would lose her. I thought of the many times she had told me that her son had already lived longer and more fully than some doctors had believed he would, facing with tenacity the disease of his childhood and continuing daily to fight the effects of post-polio syndrome. As he spoke to me now, about family and forever, I was sure I'd still be his family on the day he entered eternity. I smiled at the positive outlook he had instilled in me. Earlier that summer as I was treading water in the lake, he was lying on the end of my dock, the evening breeze tousling his grey hair as he offered me the wisdom gathered from a long life: "All the way to heaven is heaven."

Maj said he had no fear of death. He shook his head and looked off into the distance the day he broached this unsettling topic. I couldn't deny my fear, so I hoped that one day, after acquiring as much experience and learning as he had, that I, too, would be able to accost this most basic fear with the valor that Maj displayed. I thought back to the words of a poem by Edward Fitzgerald that Maj had urged me to consider and had continued to reference time and time again:

> *Come fill the Cup, and in the fire of Spring*
> *Your Winter-garment of Repentance fling:*
> *The Bird of Time has but a little way*
> *To flutter—and the Bird is on the Wing.*

It was clear to me that this was more than a stanza of a poem. For Maj, it had become a life motto. He said he didn't fear death, but he constantly returned to these words about the brevity of life. I wished that I could face mortality without fear while remembering that my life was but a vapor. In true Maj fashion, he soon proposed a precept that helped me understand the connection between living life and accepting eternity. He quoted a poem by William Blake that he had mentioned to me early in our conversations:

> *He who binds himself to a joy*
> *Does the winged life destroy*
> *He who kisses the joy as it flies*
> *Lives in eternity's sunrise*

As I began to accept this idea of loving with an open hand, he proudly added another epithet, *Joy Kisser*, to the growing list of nicknames he had bestowed upon me. By now, I had acquired quite a collection of monikers from Maj: *Joy Kisser, Talia, Brave-Heart, Dream Catcher, Silkie, Rosebud.* My real name was a thing of the past. I associated with my birth name the pain of my history, the people who didn't know the real me, and a life I wanted to leave behind. Maj's beliefs were encapsulated in a refusal to bind himself to Joy. Instead, he would receive Joy with a kiss and let it pass as it flies away with the Bird of Time, a bird none of us can avoid. It made sense to me. Death is inevitable, and enjoying life seemed a sensible way to pay respect to the sanctity of our short time on this earth. But at the time I had not heeded the entire teaching.

Your Winter-garment of Repentance fling

Maj would have to fling the winter garment of repentance in order to fill his Cup. This was the crux. I regret that I did not see it sooner.

The end of therapy was nowhere near the end of my thinking about the problems that had brought me to where I had found myself. My mind had become trapped in a box. As time ticked by, bringing me closer to the trip, Maj tried to help me unlock my mind. He said there were so many different ways to find yourself, to respond to the life you could choose to live, to express yourself. He didn't understand why people continued to think that there was only one way to do these things when the possibilities were endless. Since sexual abuse was the prevalent issue for me, he applied these concepts to that area of my life, reminding me that I could reclaim what I felt had been taken. After all, he reasoned, I was a sexual being, with many years ahead of me in which to enjoy my body. He said that I needed to learn to embrace my sexuality. Afterwards, my husband could participate with me in the beauty. But first, I needed to remove the unnecessary debris of shame from my mind, planted long ago in situations I did not choose and wished to erase. He suggested that I try to enjoy a sexual experience of my own choosing, in which I could maintain control.

He told me that I should touch myself. I thought back to the dock, where he had asked me to touch myself and then accepted me, literally, putting my fingers into his mouth. I had worried about his intentions at the time, but I had tried to let it go. Now, it seemed that he really was just helping me find myself. He hadn't continued to touch me. Now, he was showing me that I didn't have to be scared to touch myself, to own my sexuality, and to share what I found with my husband. I didn't want sex to be associated with fear any longer. One night as the sun was setting, I approached the empty cabin with a key in my hand. I was going to unlock my mind. I turned the key in the lock and closed the door behind me. I laid on his bed and did exactly as I'd been told.

Chapter Sixteen

"For thus says the Lord God, the Holy One of Israel:
'In returning and rest you shall be saved; in quietness and
confidence shall be your strength.' But you would not, and you said,
'No, for we will flee on horses.'"
(Isaiah 30:15-16)

It had always been clear to me that Maj was an intensely spiritual person. I was honored that a man to whom everyone turned to for guidance and advice saw something special in me and thought it worth his time. Time which he always pointed out was so brief. I felt special to receive his help. Perhaps the only thing that Maj enjoyed more than sharing the stories of his life was living in the bliss of the moments that created those stories. He told me of his spiritual studies in Colorado where he shook the hand of a nun who sent a lightning bolt through him as they touched. The electricity, he said, was undeniable. He spoke of God and prophets, opening my mind to the wisdom he had acquired, much of it, long before I was born. I reciprocated by offering him what I was learning from the Bible. When I quoted Psalms to him, he said that it was easy to see where the first great poetry had originated. He reminded me that we were living in the moments that created great poetry, beautiful stories, and a shared life. I thanked him for introducing me to deep water, as he taught me what it meant to find peace.

I was walking through a Christian bookstore one day when I saw a painting that looked just like his pier, a boat floating in the stillness of the water beside it. At the top of the painting were the words *In quietness and trust is your strength-- Isaiah 30:15*. I bought the picture for him as a symbol of my gratitude. His powers of imagination and expression were alluring, perhaps contagious. He assured me that I held the same abilities, and that he saw them in me. In earlier days, R had suggested that I write down my dreams as part of my psychotherapy with him. Now, with R gone, Maj asked me to tell my dreams to him. It was my dreams and nightmares that gave Maj a peek into my imagination and expression, and he interpreted the images and metaphors found in the realms of my subconscious. He was enthralled with exploring the uncharted parts of me, that latent potential that he could see coming to fruition. Maj said he wasn't a dreamcatcher like me. He woke from his rest with no

memory of his dreams. But he had already taught me that though
much was hidden, it was always nearby.

As I prepared to leave the lake and make the journey to visit
Maj's mother, I felt for the first time in a long time that it was
possible for me to feel whole again. Maj sensed it. Shortly before I
left home, he wrote to me:

*Beautiful, this new life emerging, lifting you up with it. This
is what you wanted, this life that was alive, not the old
entanglements, the life tied to the past, but one that belonged to you,
was, is you. You are becoming who you really are, that unfolding.
You will be this way forever now. The bird will never return to the
cage. You are absolutely not broken nor frail. You are uncharted. If
you could see yourself, you would be astonished. You are worth a
kingdom. I know, this is the truth, you are whole and shining.*

With that, I hugged my husband and son goodbye and got
into a car with Greg and Bradley. Five hundred miles later, I arrived
in a different world. No lake or globe. Just a hungry spirit waiting
for me, in a quiet house on a dead-end street.

It was late when we arrived at Maj Ragain's home. The moon
pierced through the darkness as we parked in the driveway and
climbed the steps to a front porch encased by glass windows and a
friendly sign reminding friends and visitors to remove their shoes
before entering the house. I stepped into the front room and saw him
lying on a soft blue mat spread out over a plush white carpet in front
of a brick fireplace, his fingers laced together over a book with the
title *Buddha's Brain* opened in front of him as he relaxed in his den.
On his left, a silver platter held a tall goblet of pomegranate juice
from which he drank. On his right was a large portrait of himself
hanging on the wall. The room was illuminated only by a small lamp
on the floor beside the area where he lay. Seeing him in his natural
habitat, I had the distinct feeling that I was entering some strange
mix of a king's quarters and a wild animal's lair. We were on his
territory, and as always, his presence commanded our attention.

Everyone exchanged greetings. As my fellow travelers
stooped to shake the hand of our friend, I saw Maj slide money
across the floor to Greg who said, "Alright, so are we square now?"
Maj nodded affirmatively. Greg later told me that he had promised to
come and visit Maj on another occasion but was unable to keep the

promise. Greg was making up for that debt with this visit, and Maj had offered to pay for the gas for the trip. As Maj's wife entered to greet all of us, I sat on the brown leather couch, under the picture of Maj's face. I said hello to Maj and his wife as Bradley and Greg returned to the car to carry in our luggage. Maj's wife offered us refreshments. I requested pomegranate juice since Maj had already told me what to drink. After putting our bags away, I sat down on the floor in front of the couch. Maj's wife lay next to him beside the blue mat, and the guys took seats in the living room with us after finding the blow-up mattresses that Maj had offered them. They would be setting up their beds in the living room, but there was a guest room at the end of the hall for me. After hours of storytelling and catching up, Maj's wife retired to their bedroom. The rest of us continued to visit well into the night until I excused myself to change my clothes and prepare for bed.

After changing from my rumpled travel clothes and into a pair of grey leggings, leg warmers, and an oversized pink t-shirt, I opened the door to walk down the hall and use the restroom before going to bed for the night. When I opened the door, Maj was sitting on the hardwood floor in the hallway right in front of my bedroom door. I looked down at him, then my eyes rose over him to see the bathroom door behind him. Further down the hall I saw the closed door of the bedroom where his wife was sleeping. As my eyes returned to him, he smiled. The silence was awkward as I waited for him to speak or move so that I could go to the bathroom. He looked back at the threshold that led to the dining room and living room where we could hear Greg and Bradley talking. When he looked at me again, he motioned with his right hand for me to come toward him.

"Kiss me," he ordered.

The feeling I had experienced on the dock, when I had obeyed him the first time, returned. I was filled with confusion at being asked to cross this uncomfortable line by the person I respected and trusted most in the world. My heart began to race as I tried to discern how to handle such a proposition. I was cornered in front of the guest bedroom. I actually imagined stepping over my crippled friend's body, but that seemed so terribly impudent that I could never bring myself to do it. In an attempt to both appease my conscience and submit to his request, I leaned down and put my lips to his right cheek. As I returned to my standing position and waited for him to scoot himself down the hallway, he stared at me, unsatisfied.

"No," he said.

The silence that followed was more uncomfortable than the first. We were in a stare down, as if we were waiting to see who would blink first.

He lasted longer.

In capitulation, I knelt down before him and kissed his lips. His hand gripped the back of my neck as I started to pull away, but not before his tongue found its way deep into my mouth. When he released me, he made a groaning noise and laughed quietly under his breath. With an approving smile he whispered, "Goodnight Talia," before moving down the hall and returning to his den.

I quickly went to the bathroom and then hurried back down the hall, climbing into bed and pulling the covers up to my chin. I thought of my husband. I thought of my son. I took my bottle of Xanax off of the nightstand, poured a half-dozen pills into my mind, and closed my eyes.

Chapter Seventeen

"They are the enemies of the cross of Christ: whose end is destruction, whose god is their belly, and whose glory is in their shame."
(Philippians 3:18-19)

The next morning, I woke to the smell of pancakes and coffee. I joined everyone for breakfast and completed my ritual of cutting my food into small pieces and pushing it around my plate. Maj's wife left for the nursing home to bring Maj's mother back to the house for the day. I couldn't wait to see her. I also couldn't believe that my trip had already taken such a turn. I had known that I would be staying at Maj's house, but I knew that it was his wife's house as well. I also thought that it was good that I had both Greg and Bradley with me. But in the hallway the night before, none of that had mattered. Maj had asked for something from me, and I had given it to him, again. I knew that I would never be able to keep that secret from my husband, and I was swimming in guilt. When I went to my guestroom to get ready for the day and my reunion with Maj's mother, I dug down to the bottom of my duffel bag and found the cough medicine that I had packed. I took what I hoped was enough to numb my feelings without making it obvious to anyone that I was high.

Maj's mother arrived, pushing a walker that I had never seen her use, but she was still the same beautiful, strong, and loving woman that I knew. Her white hair was curled, rouge accented her cheekbones, and she smiled as brilliantly as I had always remembered when I hugged her. I sat next to her on the couch, thankful to be making the most of the reason for our trip. She asked what else we planned to do while we were in town, and Maj began making suggestions for places to visit and possible adventures. Of the different suggestions, the guys decided they'd like to explore some natural areas and perhaps do some hiking. Soon, Maj's wife was grabbing windbreakers from the coat closet, and when she was out of earshot Maj looked at me and said, "You'll be staying here." Clearly, Maj could not join them, but his mother couldn't either. I had made the trip to visit her, so I was happy with staying behind to gain more time with her.

As Maj's wife was handing out the jackets, she asked me,

"Are you coming?" I was uncomfortable rejecting her offer, but it had already been decided.

"No thanks, I think I'm going to stay here."

She said okay, and the three of them left. The three of us who remained continued talking in the living room. Until Maj decided to change that.

"Mom, you look pretty tired. Don't you want to go into the guest room and take a nap?"

She took a deep breath and said, "Oh, sure, I guess I could lay down for a little while." She leaned on her walker, and I walked with her as she labored slowly down the hall under the pain of her healing hip. After making sure that she was resting comfortably, I returned to the living room.

While Maj and I were talking, he moved away from his blue mat and sat next to me on the floor by the couch. As the conversation progressed over the next half-hour, he returned to some conversations we had previously by phone. He mentioned the episode of masturbation, and while I didn't feel particularly comfortable talking about it, I couldn't deny that it had happened. Then he began talking about how he imagined I looked down there while reaching toward me and pulling the waistband of my tights from my body with two crooked fingers, saying that he wanted to see my pubic hair. He looked down my pants and then put my waistband back in place, but as he did, he ran his hand between my legs and began rubbing my crotch on the outside of my pants.

I was uncomfortable. I was 500 miles away from home in an unfamiliar house in a city I had never visited. In retreat, I scooted myself backwards until my back was against the front of the couch, but there was nowhere else to go, so I stopped resisting. I didn't say no, and I never asked him to stop. Consequently, my body began responding to the continuous touch, and Maj whispered that he could tell I was turned on.

Suddenly, we heard the bedroom door open, and his mother started down the hallway. Almost as if nothing had happened, I stood and helped her back to the couch.

Later that night, before a dinner of eggplant parmesan prepared by Maj's wife, I called home to my husband and Abram. I felt like the worst mother in the world while Abram babbled sweetly into the phone. I wanted to get everything off my chest, but I couldn't imagine what kind of position I would put everyone in if I suddenly blurted out that Maj and I had kissed, that he had touched me intimately on the living room floor, and that I knew something bad was happening but I was not stopping it. I worried that if I confessed this to my husband, on the phone no less, that he would tell me that he didn't want to be with me. Before I left for my trip, I had a brief conversation with my husband about Maj. I tried to relieve some of my guilt about Maj's actions on the dock. I could not bring myself to confess, fully, what Maj had told me to do, but I did try to tell him that Maj had crossed some lines.

"Maj doesn't always keep his hands to himself," I told my husband while we were standing in the kitchen putting away dishes.

As before, when I tried to tell him about the awkward hug Maj had given me, my husband still could not believe that there was a problem. He still insisted that Maj was harmless. An old man in a wheelchair. My husband had given me a half-smile and rolled his eyes as if to say, "Boys will be boys."

No, I didn't think I could announce this over the phone, not when I couldn't even come home yet. Greg had driven us there, and I was not about to tell him or Bradley what was happening. I knew I was stuck there for the next few days until we left at the planned time. I would just have to endure the guilt for the next couple of days, until I returned home. Then I could tell my husband that there was something wrong with me. I couldn't seem to stand up for myself.

I married my husband because he had felt safe to me. I had learned that I could never be safe on my own. Too many times I had said no to men, and my body had been sexualized anyway. Those times left me terrified of being exploited, betrayed, raped again. I would rather submit to a sexual act than risk feeling overpowered. I had been out of control for a long time, and my obedience to Maj's demands was merely a way for me to feel like I had some control, that he was not dominating me. But that was an illusion. He had dominated me. He had wooed me with trust and commitment. By this point, I knew that what Maj was doing was wrong, but I could not say no.

I ended my conversation with my husband and then took more cough medicine and Xanax before joining everyone for the evening meal.

After dinner, I rode in the car with Maj's wife to return his mom to her room at the nursing home. When we returned back to the house, we all stayed up late talking again. Once again, Maj made me feel special, like he always had. He handed me some colorful stones and told me to keep them. "They've got some magic," he told me. He often gave me things that had belonged to him, pictures, books, and now, stones. He looked through my journal and pulled out my bookmark, which was a piece of white paper folded in half, a photocopied guide to reading through the Bible in a year. The paper was riddled with inked checkmarks and small notes of verses I had read. I had been reading the Bible all year long and only had three months left. I couldn't help but notice that when he saw it, his face revealed disappointed confusion. I remembered a time when he asked me on a Sunday evening what I had learned at church that night. He said that he thought whatever I learned there could be learned at the lake. At the time, I had just smiled, thinking that God surely would teach us wherever we were.

After looking through my journal, he showed me the journal that he had decided to start keeping. He had told me that he had been inspired by the time and effort I took to record my thoughts and experiences. As I flipped through the journal, I found an old black-and-white photo of him. He was propped up on crutches, and the back brace that he sometimes wore was around his midsection. He wore a sleeveless undershirt and denim jeans. His face was serious, and he held up a fist, as if threatening whoever dared to catch his stare. He said his friend had taken the photograph and entitled it *The Pugilist*. He tore the picture from the hard-backed journal and told me to take it home with me. As I closed the journal, I noticed a picture glued to the inside cover of the book. It was a printed picture of an old painting: a woman receiving oral sex.

Chapter Eighteen

"If a man is found lying with a woman married to a husband, then both of them shall die—the man that lay with the woman, and the woman; so, you shall put away the evil from Israel."
(Deuteronomy 22:22)

The following day I drank a lot of cough medicine. My memory of that day isn't very clear, but I know that it was Sunday and that Maj's wife and the guys were around. Maj's friend, who sometimes visited the cabin with him, also came to visit. I'm a bit of an acrobat, and at the lake Maj had enjoyed watching me do back walkovers in the yard and cartwheels off the dock. He had learned the names of some of my stunts, and as we sat visiting in the living room with Greg, Bradley and his friend, he asked me to entertain them.

"Show these boys a *valdez*, Talia."

From my seated position on the carpet, I straightened my left leg out and in front of me, and in one fluid motion I arched my back and lifted my left leg into the air, holding myself up with my arms and kicking my legs over until I was in a standing position, being careful not to kick any of the men in the crowded room. The guys were obviously impressed by my litheness. I saw Maj look at his friend with a huge smile before dropping his head and laughing at his friend's speechless and shocked reaction. I knew that I was Maj's puppet, controlled by the strings of attachment that had formed when I opened up to him about my private suffering and became dependent on my relationship with him.

Monday morning, the last full day of our trip, Maj's wife had to return to her job, and I was looking forward to my plans to visit Maj's mom in the nursing home that day. When I woke and stepped into the hallway, she was already gone, and I heard my middle name whispered from behind the cracked door of Maj's bedroom. I stepped into his room to answer his call. He told me to close the door behind me. I sat on the floor in front of the bed where he lay. We talked for a while before he touched the first layer of my clothing and said, "Take that off." I removed the t-shirt, thankful that I had layered it over a tank top, but my relief was short-lived. When he saw the undershirt, he looked into my eyes again and said, "Another layer." I started to shake, aware that he was not afraid to ask for this to go too far, and I had proven myself incapable of telling him no.

During a phone conversation he had once said to me, "I don't think you know the word *no*." At the time, his requests had been less crucial, or so I thought. Now, as I sat cross legged at the edge of his mattress on the floor, I knew that my inability to deny his instructions was going to cause me great guilt, shame, and pain. I removed my tank top and self-consciously looked at the thin bra that was the only article of clothing left between my nakedness and his twisted desire. Leaning towards me, he said again, "Another layer." I fixed my eyes on the floor and pulled the last garment over my head, holding it in my hands. As he started kissing my chest, I wished that he could just love me with my clothes on. His fondling of me was as slow and deliberate as the words he had used to establish trust within me in the first place.

When he told me to take my leggings off, I gave him a pleading look that was ignored, but he later told me that he would never forget the hesitant look on my face because it did not match my actions. I waited for his next instruction. When he told me what to do, my mind flashed back to the image of the woman in the back of his journal. He told me to get on his bed and sit in a position so psychologically uncomfortable to me that while I tried to obey, I kept breaking the posture he demanded. Repeatedly, he told me to return to the position he had instructed me. I couldn't get my mind and body to cooperate, and I felt like a disappointment to him. He reassured me, though, saying that he could see that my flower was finally opening to him. I had never understood that *this* was how I was going to bloom into a better life. While my mind was still swirling with the long history of flower talk, blooming, and my nickname, *Rosebud*, he referred to me in that moment as an animal in heat. My eyes found the floor once more as he compared my genitalia to that of a mare waiting to be inseminated.

From the next room, we began to hear Bradley and Greg stirring. I moved to his left side, but he quickly told me to get back on the floor. I realized I had touched his wife's side of the bed. Again, I felt that I had done something to upset him. I put all of the layers of my clothes back on and stood to leave before one of the guys could arrive at Maj's door. When I reached the door, Maj told me to stop and come back.

"Check the bed for Talia hairs," he said.

Mortified, I leaned over him and inspected the white sheets for my own hair, so that his advances toward me would not be discovered by his wife.

I joined Greg and Bradley in the living room, but it wasn't long before Maj's friend showed up to take them elsewhere, and we were alone again. By this point, I had figured out that Maj had arranged this in advance. Still, I took comfort in knowing that Maj's mother was expecting me to come to the nursing home with Maj that day. Throughout the day, Maj's mother, my friend that I had traveled to see, called both the house phone and Maj's cell phone in anticipation of our arrival to visit her. Maj ignored the calls. I listened to the recording of his answering machine pick up call after call. He said nothing. My heart dropped with the realization of his coldness towards his mother and my guilt that I was unable to go see her.

When I had first accepted Greg's offer to make the trip, Maj had invited me to attend one of the poetry classes he taught at the university. That class would take place later that evening. I had honestly believed that would be the only time that I was alone with him, but I had spent a considerable amount of time alone with him by this point, and each encounter had altered my world. I wasn't the same person that had arrived on his doorstep. I was changed.

Maj had taught me so much about self-actualization in the years since I had first met him. Over the course of the past three days, it was as if he were finally rejoicing in seeing me reach the potential that he had always believed I had. I was so confused. My relationship with him seemed to have become closer, but it was alienating me from everyone else around me. I knew my conscience would never allow me to keep everything that had happened a secret. I thought my husband would hate me when I told him all that had taken place. I feared that he would leave me. I couldn't imagine how I would survive such a loss. Maj was the only person in my life who knew everything about me. As the case had been for quite some time, he would be the only person I could turn to for support. Maybe what he had said about remembrance and living on through a relationship was true. Maybe my relationship with him was the only thing keeping me from self-destructing. The dock, the kiss in the hallway, him touching me in the living room and seeing me naked in his bedroom played out in my mind as one uninterrupted scene. I tried to imagine what someone might think if they found out what a twenty-eight-year-old girl had done with a seventy-three-year-old man. I didn't even understand it. I was sure that Maj was the only one who did. I was in way over my head. Months earlier, on the dock, I had decided that I could not cope with the threat of him abandoning me. Apparently, I was willing to do anything to avoid that. In many ways, I felt that I already had.

I had entered Maj's home unaware that it was harvest season. He had taken great care in planting a seed, watering it, and watching it grow. Perhaps I had become a rose. Maybe I was beautiful. But if you love a flower, you should not pick it. On the living room floor that day, Maj penetrated me. When you pick a flower, it begins to die. So, it was with me.

After, he put an Iris Dement album in the CD player. I had never heard of the singer before, but he was sure that I would like it. She was another of the faithful women on whom Maj had a crush. He described meeting her in person but said he didn't think she liked him much. My shame over what had just happened overwhelmed me as her voice came through the speakers.

> *I'm glad Jesus came, glory to His name,*
> *Oh, what a friend is He.*
> *He so freely gave His own life to save,*
> *From bonds of sin set free.*

I couldn't believe that he was playing gospel music for me after what he had just done to me on the living room floor. The song continued.

> *Nobody knows what it means to me,*
> *Nobody knows but my God and me.*
> *I've got that old-time religion in my heart*
> *And it's way down inside.*

He was right in thinking that I'd connect to the songs. The lyrics, "*Nobody knows but my God and me,*" reminded me not only of my faith, but also of the fact that I was not alone in that house with Maj. Whatever secret had been created between Maj and me was not a secret kept from God. I knew that what was happening was wrong, and I took comfort in knowing that He knew. Maj gave me a copy of the Iris Dement album to take home with me. The title was *Lifeline*. I played the entire album on repeat for months to come.

For lunch, I poured cereal into bowls from the box that his wife had left on the floor for him. He ran his silver spoon between my toes before dipping into his bowl and shoveling a spoon-full of corn flakes into his mouth. I did my best to smile and carry on with the day despite the pain that I felt and my fear of returning home to my husband and son. After we ate, I ran a bath and washed myself in the tub. Gospel songs continued to play in the background. As I was drying off, I heard him yell to me not to drain the tub. To my surprise, he bathed in my dirty water. Once he had dragged himself naked into his bedroom, I retrieved the collared shirt that he was unable to reach in his closet. He reached up my dress and touched my butt as I did so. It seemed useless to reject any of his advances at this point. He had been inside me, and he continuously reminded me of that. He replayed that moment, that had lasted only seconds, over and over again in his mind and out loud to me.

That night on the way to Maj's poetry class, we stopped by the nursing home for only a few minutes. I went in and pushed his mom out to the car in her wheelchair, shielding her eyes from the bright sun. After returning her to her room and telling her goodbye for the last time, I joined him again in his car.

"Tearful goodbye?" he asked.

I didn't answer. He drove to the university using the modified apparatus that allowed him to drive his car with his hands. Between stop lights, he rested his hand on my thigh. When we arrived, I helped him from the car and entered the school I went to his office with him, meeting his friends and colleagues along the way. After meeting a woman friend of his, he mentioned that he thought she was aware of what was going on between us.

As we walked into his classroom, he told me that the tables were set up in a square and told me to sit on the other side of the room from him. This way, he'd be able to have a good view of me. He laughed as he said that I could spread my legs and flash him under the table. That evening during the poetry class I observed him in his role of compassionate teacher. The same reverence that he held in my neighborhood was evident in all of his interactions with students and co-workers. When the class ended, I pushed his wheelchair for the first and only time as we returned to his car and then to his home, where Greg, Bradley, and his wife were waiting for us.

The next morning, we rose early to make the long trip back to the lake. Maj stayed in his bed, but I sat next to him on the floor, dreading my departure. Greg and Bradley came in to shake his hand before leaving. After starting the car and arranging our bags, I walked back into his bedroom to tell him goodbye. I was afraid to leave him. I could not conceive of returning to my life with the additional baggage I was now carrying.

"You came back," he said, in a pleased, warm voice.

I bent down and gave him a hug, as a tear rolled down my face. I was incredibly hurt and hopelessly attached to him.

On the long drive home, I prepared myself for confession. Vows that I had sincerely made had been overridden by my insatiable need for help and Maj's unorthodox plan for my healing. Devastated, I felt myself slipping into a pit of darkness. Parts of me were starting to decay as my mind began to absorb the stark reality of what had taken place and the consequences that might follow. How badly I had wanted to never feel the powerlessness of being dehumanized by a man again. How great the desire to find help and not be abandoned.

My phone rang twice on that drive home. The first time, it was my husband. He called to tell me that his father had suffered a heart attack and was in the hospital. The second was Maj. He called to check on me and assure me, as he always did, that he was nearby and looking forward to talking to me once I got home. The first call served to multiply my guilt, and I decided that I could not further my husband's stress by walking into our house and asking him for help, confessing the details of my experience to alleviate my own emotional state while damaging his. The second call allayed my abandonment fears and intensified my sick need for companionship from the man who was treating my psychological dysfunction with the very behaviors that had caused it. I felt myself catapulted into a death spiral, unsure of what it would take to stop the madness before I lost control entirely and hit the ground.

I never returned home. I did reach the lake and the house built of walls and beams, but I was faced with the fact that the delicate globe from my childhood that I had tried desperately to recreate was in fact, imaginary. There was nothing protecting me from the dangers of the outside world. It is all the outside world. There were no boundaries. I no longer felt that I deserved to call the tall house on the lake that I shared with my husband and son, *home*. It was just a house. As we pulled into the driveway, I opened the door before the car even rolled to a stop, bounding past my husband to hug my son. Though my husband had expected me to look forward to reuniting with our boy, his face showed disappointment as I passed him by without even stopping for a hug. I felt awful when I realized that I had avoided him, but I knew that his disappointment in me was only going to get worse.

Chapter Nineteen

"But there were also false prophets among the people . . . "
(II Peter 2:1)

Over the next two months, my condition worsened. I restricted food, took DXM to numb my feelings, and drank alcohol for the first time since I had gotten pregnant. Maj offered to pay for me to enter a treatment center for eating disorders, but I was sure that wouldn't help under the circumstances. With Christmas approaching, Maj told me that his son and granddaughters were coming to visit over the holidays and warned me that he probably wouldn't contact me during that time. Isolated and depressed, a couple of days after Christmas, I overdosed. Feeling anxious and hopeless, I had swallowed a handful of Xanax after drinking nearly a liter of wine. Afraid that I wouldn't wake up if I fell asleep, I woke my husband and told him what I had done. Because he had to wake up very early the next morning to go to work, his frustration was apparent. I told him that I would call my sister for help, and he drifted back to sleep. Minutes later, my brother-in-law showed up at my door to take me to the hospital. This was not the intervention I had expected.

I arrived in the emergency room just before midnight, hoping the professionals would understand that something was clearly wrong, that I needed help. I lay in a bed staring at a poster on the wall with a pain scale of one to ten with round faces ranging from a smile to a look of anguish. *Ten*, I thought. *I'm a ten.* A counselor from a local crisis center arrived and began asking me questions.

"Do you feel that you have sufficient support from friends and family?" she asked.

I looked at my brother-in-law and back at the counselor. "No."

When asked about my current stressors, I reported that I felt negatively about almost every area of my life, including work, family, and all of my relationships. The hospital called poison control and released me in less than an hour. The professionals had provided all the help that they would. I returned to my house, slept for a few hours, and attended part of the Sunday morning service at my church the next day. My nose bled off and on the entire next day, and I had a migraine that lasted into the next week. After this failed attempt to receive help from a hospital, I began to feel that I couldn't receive help from anyone.

Maj resumed talking to me when his visit with his family over the holidays had ended. I felt suicidal by this point, and I told both my mother and my husband that I wanted to die. Maj showed great concern, and he hesitated as he brought up a name I never imagined he would mention again.

"What would R tell you to do?" he questioned.

I had forgotten that when I accepted R's offer to treat me by phone, I rejected the idea of accepting his referral to his colleague across the hall. He had suggested this yet again when we spoke for the last time.

"He'd tell me to make an appointment with the man across the hall from his old office," I said.

Maj, aware that he could not protect me from my own impulses, suggested that I follow R's advice. That afternoon I dialed the number of the clinical psychologist R had recommended. I expected to reach his secretary and had prepared myself for the likely possibility that he would not have any available openings. A deep voice came across the line.

"This is Dr. Cole."

Caught off guard, I hurriedly told him that I had been a patient of R, that I was having an increasingly difficult time since his retirement, and that I had hoped I could schedule an appointment. His voice was calm and reassuring.

"Yes, we can do that. Do you work outside the home?"

I let him know that I did, but I was so afraid of myself by that point that I added that I would take personal time off of work if it would help me get an appointment. I was desperate. After agreeing on an appointment time, I hung up the phone. I later found out that I had filled his last available opening.

Maj and I now talked on the phone almost every day. His good morning greeting by email was as routine as his coffee, and he would always arrange a time to phone me later in the day. These conversations were indicative of the compromise that had been formed. Maj talked to me about my life, my health, and my problems, but at some point in the conversation, he always began to relay his sexual fantasies and asked me to masturbate. He told me of the sexual conquests and adventures of his past, including losing his virginity to a prostitute and receiving oral sex from a man. Perversely, not absent from these conversations was talk of spirituality and faith. It was during this time, however, that I could no longer bring myself to assume that he was talking about the same Lord to whom I prayed when he said the word *god*. His requests and the nature of our relationship were so distant from what felt right and moral to me that I could not keep from wondering about a strange coincidence that had occurred just after I had opened up to him about my past.

Maj had called me to talk about the long letter that I had written to him about my abuse. I thanked him for talking with me about the rape, saying that I knew it was a heavy topic.

"It's not heavy for me," he assured. "Load me up. I'll carry it. I'll be your wheelbarrow." I smiled as I hung up the phone, thankful for his willingness to bear my burdens with me. At that very moment, I turned on the television, the voice of Charles Stanley, a television preacher, filled my living room:

"You could be sailing through the woods and through the mountains on a clear track and you're over here with a wheelbarrow trying to make things work. You'll get off track. Now remember this: when you acknowledge that He's in absolute control, you have acknowledged an awesome sense of faith. I'm trusting you, God, for everything."

The synchronicity certainly gave me pause. It was undeniable. I knew that trusting God above all else was central to my faith, but I also considered the fact that we do have to allow other people into our lives. It's part of the nature of our existence. I felt certain that Maj was helping me in some way. I believed that I was trusting in God and that there were a few people in my life, like Maj and R, who were doing their best to help me along the way. At this point, Maj had never done anything to alert me to any kind of a problem. So, I continued stumbling through the woods with him. Now, as I waited for my first appointment with a new shrink, I knew I had gotten off track.

Frail in body, mind, and spirit, confused beyond explanation, and clinging to a death drive that promised relief, I set off for my first appointment with Dr. Jack Cole. His name means *God is gracious*. I believe it was unmerited favor that allowed me to find my way into his office that day. Dr. Cole opened his door and took a step back, inviting me into his office. He was tall and thin, a decade older than myself, and wore a blue button-up shirt and striped tie.

His confidence and poise was a reassuring contrast to my diffident self-consciousness. I walked past him and found my seat in a chair across from his. He took his seat and smiled warmly.

"What can I help you with?" he asked.

I began to describe my recent emergency room visit, trouble eating, and feelings of hopelessness. To say that he listened is an understatement. It was more like he was studying me. Every expression, my struggle to make eye contact, each word that I said or hesitated to say, the movement of my body--I had the distinct feeling that nothing was going unnoticed. His own posture rarely changed, but neither did his attentiveness or focus. I felt like I was under a microscope, but because I needed so badly for him to see to the bottom of my pain, it was comforting. Avoiding eye contact, I told him I had been raped. He actually said very little with words, allowing the silences to permeate the room until I shared the next thing that was on my mind, but his attention and his eyes spoke throughout the appointment. As the hour came to an end, he told me that he looked forward to working with me. I left, hopeful that he would be able to help me, but carrying secrets that were eroding my will to live.

Each day my conversations with Maj became more sexual and more spiritual. He was hell-bent to release my sexuality, and I was determined to understand what kind of god it was that he had been mentioning since the beginning of our relationship, many years now in the past. Surely the common ground on which I had believed we were walking existed still. It often seemed as though it did. Maj referred to me as a child of God, but his view of the divine and eternity was beginning to sound less and less familiar to what I believed. I wanted to understand how all the different sides of the things he was saying fit together.

"Odd how the different facets of us present themselves as we turn the jewel in hand," he wrote. "I want to protect you, to circle you with loving attention, whispering, *trust*, and *believe*."

But he also told me that the spiritual and the erotic path were one in the same. He said wisdom could be found through desire. This revelation mystified me, but he had been reminding me for quite some time that nobody would ever relish me the way that he did, and I was beginning to believe that were true. I never stopped wanting his acceptance, and I never had to wait long for him to assure me that I had it. He spoke to my insecurities frequently. I went to bed at night with fresh affirmations of his acceptance of me:

"Women such as you--and I don't expect to know another--are so special that you elude judgment or understanding. You simply must be accepted. That is what I have done. Sweet dreams, Talia."

Meanwhile, his imaginative world of myth in which I had been created as a Silkie began to grow and transform. He called himself a dragon. He said that people who are afraid of dragons are fearful of their own unconscious lives and of energies within themselves that they cannot control. Fearful of the dragons within themselves, weak people hide themselves within their small worlds and die there. He was grateful that I was not like those frightened people.

"Look around you, Baby," he encouraged me. "Then, look at yourself and what you have done, and are doing, and about to do again."

I lived in the fantasy as best I could, but I soon realized that deviating from his storyline was growing increasingly difficult. One afternoon as we spoke, my tone was flat and my voice hesitant. When he asked me what was wrong I said that I was still bothered by things in my past. To my shock, Maj's voice was raised as he barked angrily into the phone.

"Oh, your past! Everyone has a past! When I was in the hospital as a kid, a priest tried to suck my cock. I kicked him and told him to go away and he moved on to the next kid!"

I stood silently on my balcony overlooking the water, the phone to my ear, afraid to speak to the buried past he had suddenly unearthed. I felt selfish for all of my complaints about sexual abuse. His calm and soothing voice returned as he changed the subject quickly, back to our world of Spirit Lake where a dragon lived in a cabin next door and a Silkie wandered the shore in search of love. The message was clear. He did understand what it was like to be taken advantage of, but he had moved past it, and so could I. Even clearer was the implication that we would never discuss what he had said again.

Chapter Twenty

"No one speaking by the Spirit of God calls Jesus accursed, and no one can say that Jesus is Lord except by the Holy Spirit."
(I Corinthians 12:3)

It was nearing the end of winter in my now globeless world, but the snow continued to fall. I remembered Maj's claim to have no fear of death, but I was becoming more fearful of his eternal security with each conversation I had with him. On one of the final days of winter, in early March, he asked me to park in a cemetery and touch myself while he relayed all of his sexual yearnings to me. He said the experience was an intersection of love and death. I began to cry. Finally, I told him that I was afraid for his soul.

"Are you scared for me because I don't accept Jesus as my Savior?" he asked, sardonically.

I told him that I was, and then he posed another question. "I've accepted Jesus Christ as my savior three times and been baptized three times, is that enough?"

I continued to cry as he spoke softly into the phone once more. "Oh, it's sweet that you are crying for my soul. You think my soul is in jeopardy, and you are weeping. That is beautiful."

He stayed on the phone until I could be quieted. He said that we were talking in a way that we never had before, that we were moving beyond where we had been into something bigger, deeper. He thanked me for my outpouring of love for him and said that my tears blessed him. It was my youth, he said, that caused me to see difference instead of commonality in our spiritual beliefs, but he assured me that as I continued to bloom and grow, what I came to believe would be not different, but more complete.

I left the graveyard and went home to journal about all that Maj and I had discussed. As I wrote the date above my journal entry, I realized that it was R's birthday. Sadness swept over me, and I decided to do something constructive, something that would make R proud. Therapy with him had proven helpful, and I was in therapy once again, so I sat down to read a book that Dr. Cole had offered me. Knowing that I had been raped, he had loaned me a book, *Trauma and Recovery* by Judith Kerman. I began reading a chapter entitled, "The Child Grownup." As I read the words, I began to feel a panic:

"Her empathic attunement to the wishes of others and her automatic, often unconscious habits of obedience also make her vulnerable to anyone in a position of power or authority."

I heard R's voice in my head saying, "Damn it, why did Maj have to do this!"

Kerman's words continued to stun me: "The adult survivor is at great risk of repeated victimization in adult life."

The words on the page continued to shock me into reality: "Thus the victim, now grown, seems fated to relive her traumatic experiences not only in memory but also in daily life. It is not uncommon to find adult survivors who continue to minister to the wishes and needs of those who once abused them and who continue to permit major intrusions without boundaries or limits."

As the truth sank in, I began to sob and shake. I wasn't walking a path of spiritual-erotic enlightenment with Maj; I was being abused. Again.

I returned to Dr. Cole's office with the knowledge that I was, in fact, being revictimized and feeling completely powerless to stop it because Maj was the only person I trusted, who accepted me, and who promised not to abandon me. At my last appointment, I had noticed a small wooden decoration with the word *HOPE* written on it and a Bible verse beneath the word. I had a matching decoration at home with the word *PEACE* on it. I carried it with me as I crossed the floor to the red armchair and set my decoration gently on the bookcase next to the existing one. I wanted them to be together, in that office and in my mind. Dr. Cole smiled warmly at the gift.

I sat in silence, staring at the floor, which was my usual manner.

"Begin wherever you'd like," he said.

"Do you believe in God?" I asked without hesitation. "The God of the Bible," I added.

He looked solidly at me and replied, "Yes."

In that moment, I decided to stay in therapy. I decided to trust Dr. Cole. And perhaps, my trust for Maj began to diminish, slowly and painfully. I still couldn't imagine not having him in my life. After all, he had said that our relationship was born out of love. Love for his mother. The love of a family. Love for each other. But God and love cannot be separated, so I decided that the most loving thing I could do for Maj was to show him God. I would begin trying to overcome Maj's teaching with my own. Maybe I could help him see what he was missing.

Chapter Twenty-One

"He who covers his sins will not prosper, but whoever confesses and
forsakes them will have mercy."
(Proverbs 28:13)

One definition of a prophet describes a person gifted with more than ordinary spiritual and moral insight, especially an inspired teacher or poet. Just as I was deciding to witness God's truth as best I could, one such man entered my life.

As I was journaling at my office desk one day, he walked by, looking strikingly like every painting of Jesus I had ever seen. Locks of brown hair hung to his shoulders, a beard covered his handsome face, and his eyes met mine for only a moment before we both looked away. His name is Benny. He was the husband of a co-worker in my office, and I had no way of knowing by looking at him that his life was falling apart. He too, was a poet. He shared his writing on a blog he named *The Ugly Diphthong*, and due to my new interest in poetry, I soon found it. In the margin were the words, "Thanks for reading. Leave footprints." So, I did.

His writing was the kind that's difficult to stop reading. I found myself looking forward to new posts and continued leaving encouraging footprints. Knowing he had few options for connecting with other poets in our small community, I introduced him to Maj. I gave them one another's email addresses and left the first book Maj had given me, *A Hungry Ghost Surrenders His Tacklebox*, at the office for Benny to borrow the next time he visited. Maj had said that this is how the circle widens, as we write and share with one another. As it turns out, Benny was writing a book of his own, and soon I would be his audience, but Maj Ragain became his audience first.

Benny traveled to a poetry festival called *Jawbone* in Maj's town. He sat in a bookstore after a long drive one night, and Maj introduced him as the *500-mile man* who had traveled from Maj's hometown. During the open poetry reading, Maj challenged Benny to read a poem that would "drive out the devil." After shuffling through a stack of papers, Benny read a poem he had written entitled "White Man." One part of that poem reads:

In the belly of Madonna
The Savior grew strong
Without your help.
She was a better teacher,
Who never taught him
To speak with his fists.
Instead, he loved those
You paid to have sex with you
Before you stoned them.
He took nothing from them,
So, they washed his feet
With perfume and with tears.

Later that evening at a bar, Benny sat next to Maj and his wife and began making small talk. Maj's wife asked Benny if he was a friend of mine, and Maj suddenly looked away. This was Benny's first real interaction with Maj, and he felt as though there were books worth of knowledge passing between them at the mention of my name. He knew that something was off.

Maj finally began to open up to me about his true beliefs regarding God, faith, and the Bible. I learned that he never believed in original sin. He said he didn't think much about the resurrection, and he didn't know where this life ended, but there was plenty of heaven in hell for him inside of a lifetime. He taught me that the eye with which I see God is the same eye with which God sees me, and added, "If I don't tell you about Meister Eckhart, who will?" I wondered the same thing. I remember hearing that when you don't witness, you just did. If he could share his beliefs, surely I could too. Still, I felt inferior to him in every aspect of our conversations. What could I offer a man who claimed he had no fear of death?

Then an afternoon came when Maj didn't seem as fearless as he'd once claimed. Just after his wife left the house, he called me. He told me that she had been baking a pie in the oven and as it started to burn, the smoke detector in their house went off.

"I covered my head and buried my face in the carpet," he told me, "I couldn't stop screaming."

He said it was completely out of character for him to react so strongly, but that he really lost control. It was rare for me to be the one consoling him, so I listened compassionately as he admitted fear to me for the first time.

"I'm really afraid of fire. I'd like to add an exterior door to my bedroom. You never know what could happen."

It seemed fair enough that a man who couldn't walk wouldn't want to feel trapped in a back bedroom with the possibility of a fire constantly on his mind. But it was what he said next that struck me.

"I think I burned to death in a previous life," he told me gravely.

As he was thanking me for listening and telling me how important our relationship was to him, all I could think was that maybe his spiritual framework wasn't functioning to allay the most basic fear to humankind. I didn't believe that Maj had died in a fire in a previous life. I was sure that he was afraid of going to hell. It was only a few days later that I received a message conveying more of Eckhart's teaching. Maj wrote, "He said that the only thing that burns in Hell is the part of you that won't let go of your life: your memories, your attachments. They burn 'em all away. But you're not being punished, you're being freed. If you're frightened of dying, you'll see devils tearing your life away. But if you've made your peace, then the devils are really angels, freeing you from the Earth."

Maj and Benny exchanged emails. I was excited to see the two connecting, and I was happy to be forming a friendship with Benny. I had befriended his wife months before, as we worked side by side each day. I came across a poem of his about the fear of death entitled, "*Avoir de Couer.*" Part of that poem reads:

> *What cancer eats your bowels?*
> *What pain has shook your vows?*

Like me, Benny had a secret. Appreciative of the attention I was paying to his poetry, he told me that he was writing a book, and he asked if I would be his audience, providing feedback while he tried to make sense of his life through writing his story. I agreed, and he began sending me excerpts that I read and provided comments. Eventually, he reached a part of his story that he didn't feel comfortable sending through the computer, and he asked to meet me so that he could talk to me about his book.

On a Tuesday evening, I met him at a local park and got into the passenger seat of his car. As he began telling me the next part of his story, I understood why he hadn't wanted to send the information via email. He explained that his wife had been sleeping with his best friend for the past five years. It had all started one night when they began kissing in front of him, and his wife had then tried to include him in the situation. After stopping his wife from moving forward and taking her back to their bedroom, she had cried and said that she didn't want him to think that she was bad for what she already had done. After a difficult conversation, Benny returned to the room where his friend of over thirty years slept with his wife in front of him. His wife and friend included him that night, but it wasn't long before they were having sex alone, and for the past five years, he had watched from the sidelines while his wife and best friend fell in love. Afraid of losing his relationship with his three daughters, he continued to provide for his wife and daughters and maintained his friendship with the best friend he had known since they were backyard neighbors at the age of three. He was writing his book to try to make sense of it all. His best friend was also married, and his wife was expecting a child. He had decided to write the book as a sort of explanation to the unborn child about the life into which he or she was being born.

I was shocked. My heart went out to him, but I remained firmly planted in the passenger seat of his car. I couldn't fathom how I could possibly comfort someone experiencing as much pain as he had to be feeling. I saw myself in him. He felt trapped in a sexual situation that he couldn't escape. So, I said the only words I could think to say. I told him what had happened when I had taken my trip to visit Maj. We sat in the car until late that night, holding each other's secrets in our hearts. Benny gave me only one piece of advice.

"Your husband deserves to know the truth so that he can decide whether he wants to be a part of it," he said to me.

I knew he was right. While it was a relief to tell Benny what had happened, that release would only last a little while. I knew I needed help, and I knew I would have to tell someone in order to receive that help. As for Benny, he returned to his wife that night, and they made the decision to divorce.

Chapter Twenty-Two

"Sanctify them by Your truth. Your word is truth."
(John 17:17)

At my next appointment with Dr. Cole, we talked about the ways that I tried to control my state and mood with restricted eating, pills, and cutting. As I cried about the horrible events that I had told him at my first appointment, he reminded me that I was accepting guilt that didn't belong to me. My weight was starting to drop again, and Dr. Cole kept mentioning that such behavior was sometimes related to secrets that one has been asked to keep. I looked across the room at my new shrink and felt as if he were looking through me. I knew he wanted to help. I looked at the clock on the wall, watching the secondhand tick away my opportunity for full disclosure. Where would I start in explaining this to him? The day I met Maj, years ago? The day on the dock just after my first psychologist retired? My trip that I thought was planned to visit a nursing home? As the session ended, I asked if I could call him if I needed to talk. He wrote his number on my appointment reminder and smiled as he handed it to me. "Take care of yourself," he urged me.

I kept moving forward, trying to draw from my experiences. Maj shared an old Zen proverb with me: "Admire the place you are." I did my best to do just that. Between meetings at work, I went into a restaurant to order a drink. The server who handed me my order had a tattoo written in a foreign language on her wrist. I had just gotten an *A* for *Abram* tattooed on my arm in a font from a book I was reading. I decided to ask the girl what hers stood for. "Victory or death," she told me.

Maj called me on my drive home that day and I told him about the girl and her battle cry tattoo. "How about victory and death?" he retorted. Adding, "It's always both." His comment didn't set right with me, but I didn't say anything, still feeling unsure of showing disagreement with him.

As I hung up the phone, I felt discouraged and disappointed in myself for not speaking up. I sent up an unusual prayer. I asked God for a rainbow. A few minutes later, as I was driving by a large cornfield, I decided to take a picture of the dreamcatcher hanging from my rear-view mirror, the field and trees serving as a colorful background. I arrived home and decided to upload the picture to my computer. My mouth opened in awe when the photograph appeared on the screen. There was a rainbow in the center of the picture. At that moment, "Victory in Jesus" started playing from a music stream on my computer. It seemed God had just answered my prayer.

I started writing to Maj right away. I told him that victory and death was only possible with Jesus. "The resurrection is the example of simultaneous victory and death," I told him. I went on to tell him about the rainbow that I had prayed for and how it had appeared. I thought that surely, he would share in my amazement, but he never responded to that email.

A few days later, it was time for another appointment with Dr. Cole. A sign in the waiting room reminded his patients that he would be on vacation the following week. My stomach turned. The dependence that had grown when I was seeing R, then transferred to Maj, was now trying to set up camp in my new shrink's office. He opened the door and welcomed me in the inviting way that always made me feel like the office was as much mine as it was his. We were doing a lot of dream work, and as I shared my nighttime visions, it was obvious that they were full of guilt, punishment, and fear. At one point in the conversation he said, "Sometimes we do something to feel guilty consciously, so we don't have to think about the thing lurking in our unconscious mind." I shuffled in my chair and looked away, but as always, he didn't.

I changed the subject to my rainbow story. He smiled and told me it was amazing and that I should blow the picture up, frame it, and hang it in my house. As my appointment came to a close, Dr. Cole said that he knew that I lessened the degree to which things hurt me and that I hid them sometimes. He also said that he knew feeling abandonment was very hard on me and asked me to call him if I wanted--on his week off. I breathed a sigh of relief as I left.

Exhausted before bed one evening, I looked at my Bible lying on the dining room table. I almost went to bed without doing any reading but decided I should read at least a chapter before turning in for the night. I sat on the floor and opened my Bible to II Peter, chapter two. Under the heading, *False Prophets and Teachers*, were twenty-two verses filled with words describing Maj Ragain. Fear gripped my heart as I read of men who secretly bring destruction as they deny God and lead others into sensuality. "In their greed they will exploit you with false words . . . .. They have

eyes full of adultery, insatiable for sin. They entice unsteady souls."
I was reading about my own life. "For when they speak great
swelling words of vanity, they allure through the lusts of the flesh,
through much wantonness, those that were clean escaped from them
who live in error. They promise freedom, but they themselves are
slaves of corruption." As I sat alone on the floor, my Bible opened
before me, these words confronted me with truth about the danger
Maj presented. It was almost summer, and soon, Maj would be
returning to the lake.

"You invite me in when you are troubled," Maj wrote to me.
"A quiet hesitancy that I can sense even on the phone." Despite the
mounting evidence that my relationship with him was not good for
me, I continued to rely upon Maj. But my relationship with Maj was
lived forward and understood backwards. I did not yet understand
that he was a human Rorschach, willing to be whatever I wanted to
see. I had no way of knowing that after I had experienced my fantasy
of knowing a man who would accept me and my story and offer to
protect and comfort me, that his fantasies would emerge. I did not
know I'd end up a casualty of his desires.

As Maj prepared to return to Spirit Lake, he unleashed a
myriad of fantasies. "I held your wrists down; you struggled a bit . .
." his story began. With each passing day, his stories became more
intense and violent. He went from telling me that he wanted to tie me
up with a belt and leather straps to describing watching me be gang
raped in the back of a van. I sat in stunned silence as he told me that
he wanted to hit me in the face and make me bleed. I looked back at
my journey with Maj and could not understand how the conversation
had moved from "I was raped" to "I want to make you bleed."

Soon, I received a card in the mail. On the front was a poem
that he had written for the traumatized veterans to which he so
compassionately lent his time. He had masturbated into the card.

I had been ashamed by what had taken place when I was
seventeen. Every self-destructive and ill-fated attempt at dealing
with that shame had only deepened the shame that I felt. Days before
Maj returned to the cabin, he sent me the Wendell Berry poem "Do
Not Be Ashamed" once again.

> *Though you have done nothing shameful,*
> *they will want you to be ashamed.*

They will want you to kneel and weep
and say you should have been like them.
And once you say you are ashamed,
reading the page they hold out to you,
then such light as you have made
in your history will leave you.

In the beginning, he had told me that being raped should not make me feel ashamed. Now he was instructing me not to feel ashamed about our relationship, which included him telling me that he wanted to rape me. It was becoming clear to me that Maj was suggesting that the way to heal was to allow the same thing that had happened to me to happen again, but this time, to allow it and refuse to be ashamed of it. But I could not do it. The shame crawled up my body like poison ivy and wrapped itself around my neck like a noose. Maj had come to own me, and he knew it. He shared with me the *Story of O*. It is a tale of female submission, about a girl who is taught to be constantly available for any type of intercourse. He told me that at the climax of the story, the girl is presented before a large party of guests, who treat her solely as an object. He said that her submission ultimately frees her. He didn't mention that she had preferred to die.

Chapter Twenty-Three

"Deliver me from my persecutors, for they are stronger than I."
(Psalm 142:6)

Benny's story had become as clear to me as my story had become to him. We felt some relief in having uttered our ugly truths out loud. A poem for me appeared on his blog. I appreciated it. I also appreciated knowing I could continue speaking to him about the truth of what was happening with Maj, if I so chose. Maj was about to be next door once again, and I was growing frightened of my inability to resist him. I knew that I would need help in order to somehow straighten out the mess I was in. To that end, I told Dr. Cole before leaving the safety of his office one day that my relationship with Maj was sexual. I then returned to the lake, and to Maj. He had returned for his regular summer visit.

I should have confessed to my husband and spared myself the week that followed. If I had, perhaps Maj would have never made the trip. If I told my husband while Maj was next door, I am certain that the reunion of neighbors and friends would have been ruined. Both of these outcomes would have been preferable to what happened instead. Maj brought not his wife, but the best friend who had so helpfully removed Greg and Bradley from his house when we had come to visit the previous October. Maj told me that he had informed that friend of the nature of our relationship during his drive to the cabin. Like me, his friend was willing to hide Maj's secrets and remain loyal to him. Maj had shown his friend some version of the truth of what was taking place so that it would be easier for him to do as he pleased with me. He didn't have to hide what he was doing from his friend, and for an entire week I obeyed his every request with his friend serving as a sort of sentinel on Maj's behalf.

The lake was still beautiful. My neighborhood family laughed and enjoyed this magical time of year. I felt like I was the only one aware of the ugliness of the world, an ugliness that always seemed to seek me out. My husband cooked supper for everyone, serving food to the wise sage he believed was helping his wife. I did Maj's grocery shopping. I cleaned the cabin while he was fishing. I cooked his breakfast. He praised me for stepping around his pride and emptying the mason jars he used to relieve himself into in the middle of the night. I appeared wherever he told me to be, whenever he told me to be there. It took nothing more than for somebody in our company to walk away or turn their back before he was touching me, instructing me to pleasure him in some way, and degrading me with a smile on his face. However, there was one person around whom he acted especially careful.

Janet is a woman who lives just a few hundred feet further down the curvy private road that wrapped around the shoreline, and her property is the most beautiful point on the lake. Beautiful gardens brighten her vibrant yard, and her welcoming spirit makes visiting her home a serene experience. I had grown close to Janet over the previous year, often kayaking from my house to hers as a way of escape from my troubles. That summer, Maj all but shut down when Janet came around. I knew that the two had somehow known each other for many years, but I couldn't understand why Maj suddenly acted differently whenever she was around.

In truth, Maj hid his behavior from most people, but Maj didn't have to hide his behavior from the friend who had joined him on his final summer trip to the lake. Still, Maj did confess to me that his friend had suggested that he should think about what he was doing and be careful. Maj laughed when he told me this. One evening, as we stayed up late into the night to watch a meteor shower, Maj took a step forward in his brazenness that had a profound effect on me. With Greg relaxing in an armchair and Bradley taking up the couch, I sat in another chair in the quiet cabin as we talked and waited for nightfall. Maj, on the floor as always, ran his hand up the inside of my leg while he was telling the guys a story. His steady voice filled the cabin as he caressed my knee in front of them.

I remembered something Maj had said to me some time before, "I've known these boys since they were born." Nearly breathless, I looked to them to see what would happen. They both dropped their eyes and turned their heads while continuing to listen to Maj's story. He showed all of us something that night. He showed us that he was in control of all of us and that none of us would question him. He wanted me to know that my neighborhood brothers would not stop him, and he wanted them to know that I was his. When the time to go outside and star-gaze came, I came out of the restroom to find that he had sent everyone else out to the dock. He told me that he wasn't interested in the meteor shower and told me to stay in the cabin with him. Then, he made further requests.

It would be pornographic to describe the events of that week in the cabin. A confluence took place, and I lost myself. Maj had long been using the language of *we* instead of *you* and *me* to describe our relationship with each other, and I had come to accept that we had been merging into the oneness that he had predicted. Because I had felt so desperately alone, his attentions had begun as a great comfort to me. Over time, Maj had stripped me of whatever weak boundaries that I still had when I first met him, but now those boundaries were disappearing completely. The time had come for Maj's plan to reach fulfillment, for us to merge into oneness, and he was determined to see to it that we did. However, this did not come as a comfort to me. Yes, what I had once been did disappear. There was nothing left of me. I no longer felt like an individual, but I did not feel that two souls had become one. Rather, I felt my soul had left me, and my body had become an obedient prosthesis to serve Maj Ragain's fantasies.

It was too much for me to handle. At one point, I walked out of the cabin, drove to a liquor store, and poured half a bottle of vodka into my cucumber-mint lemonade before returning to him. With that, I revived a drinking problem that had lain dormant for years. On another occasion, I took out my phone and decided to text the friend to whom who I had confided my secret. I scrolled through my phone to Benny's name and typed two words: "I hurt."

Later, I learned that Benny went to confront Maj that night. I had asked Benny not to tell my husband what had been happening, and he had honored my request. Benny had hoped that confronting Maj would put an end to my suffering, but it didn't. Maj continued to use me until it was time for him to leave.

On Maj's final day at Spirit Lake, I crossed what he called our shared yard and entered the back door of the cabin. I could hear him rustling around as I crossed the kitchen and stepped into the living room. Once there, I looked to my right and saw him lying on his back, struggling to pull his pants onto his shriveled legs. I felt that I had caught him in the most vulnerable of situations. Despite Maj's limitations, he exuded both confidence and competence in the presence of others. But I, more than others, knew that deep insecurity lived just beneath the surface. Though it had not always been avoidable, Maj preferred to keep his legs covered rather than let me see the source of so much frustration, hurt, sadness, and anger. I knew that Maj would not want me to have found him struggling on the floor, out of breath, trying only to dress himself. So, I took a step back and stood quietly as the tears came to my eyes. When he had accomplished his task, I took a few steps forward into his bedroom, as if I had just arrived. He used what energy he had left to pull a denim shirt over his white undershirt, and then he looked up at me and asked for help. I knelt down before him, as I had done so many times before, and buttoned his shirt. I then rolled his sleeves halfway up his forearm, the way he preferred for them to be.

His car was already running, and all the guys were standing around outside waiting to help him into his sedan and to bid him farewell. I had come to tell him goodbye as well, but he wouldn't even look at me.

"Go home," he said.

Still sitting on the floor before him, I felt shocked at the way he had dismissed me. My mouth hung open in disbelief. As if to assure me that he was indeed being that cruel, he said it again.

"Go on. Go home."

I thought of everything that had taken place in the cabin that week. Refusing to accept his chosen punctuation to all of that hurt, I did something that demonstrates just how sick I had become. I leaned forward and hugged him. He had been manipulating me for years and using me throughout the last week. At the end of it all-- even as he was rejecting me--I tried to embrace him. But he did not hug me back. He did not tell me goodbye. I only heard him clear his throat as I crossed the cabin to the back door and disappeared. I did not know it at the time, but this unceremonious parting was our final goodbye. I would never see him again.

A few days after Maj left, I did both the hardest thing and the right thing. While my son was playing on the living room floor, I called my husband upstairs. I stood in the hallway outside our bedroom door and told him that Maj had made requests of me when I had traveled to his home back in October that I had not been able to refuse. My husband began to cry. He hung his head saying only, "It hurts so bad."

We exchanged a few pained words before he turned the corner into our bedroom and collapsed onto our bed. I covered him with a blanket. It was the death of our relationship. Our marriage was over. We would be legally divorced within a month.

Chapter Twenty-Four

"Remember, O Lord, what has come upon us; Look, and behold our reproach!"
(Lamentations 5:1)

They say every summer has a story. The story of this summer was how I lost it all. First, I lost my husband. With that, I also lost half of my precious time with my son. Then, I lost my house. My church went next. My friends stopped talking to me. And finally, I lost my job. It was a domino effect that I never saw coming. I had feared that my husband would not be able to handle what had happened, but the divorce took place in record time and left my head spinning. While the obvious thing to do was to split the time with our son, my motherly heart was not at all guarded from the pain of that rational decision. The house had to be sold, and I found myself wondering where I would live.

The pastor of my church sent me an email telling me that he was planning to use my divorce in his sermon. When I asked him not to do that, he refused. In response, I withdrew my membership from the church. Still, he persisted in his determination to humiliate me, my husband, my son, and my family in front of the congregation. I didn't understand how he could treat me so contemptuously without even bothering to ask me what had happened. He had shown more grace to my brother-in-law when he learned of his sins with no need to announce to the congregation what he had done. Nonetheless, my divorce was denounced publicly from the pulpit, with the support of the church deacons, including my brother-in-law, standing behind the pastor, united in my condemnation.

I was shocked when my friends stopped talking to me. I hadn't realized the people in my life who claimed to be best friends, who said they would love me know matter what, also had a clause in their definition of friendship that did not tolerate divorce. In addition, I lost my job because of my relationship with Benny. His wife became angry that we had begun a relationship in the midst of our separate divorces, and it wasn't long before the boss we both worked for asked me to leave.

Years later, I attended a suicide prevention training that listed some situational clues to look for in a person who might be suicidal. As I reflected on my life in the weeks following my divorce, I realized that I had experienced almost every item on the list all in a very short period. Among the clues were the loss of a cherished therapist, the loss of a major relationship, divorce, an unwanted move, loss of financial security, being fired from your job, and the fear of becoming a burden to others. I would later be asked by people how I managed not to lose my faith in God during all of this. To this day, my answer is the same. I did not look up to God and ask why I had lost so much. Instead, I looked down. I knew that the abuse, loss, and devastation that had nearly consumed my entire life were not of God. I knew there was an enemy of my soul to blame, one who had come to steal, to kill, and to destroy. The only time I looked up was to beg God for a way to move forward, beyond the suffering and shame, past the ashes of destruction. My losses, Dr. Cole later pointed out, were staggering. "There will come a time when you will want to reach back to Maj," Dr. Cole cautioned. "It is important to remember what you have lost."

I hadn't known that when I attempted to tell Maj goodbye that it would be the last time I ever saw him, but he continued to talk to me as usual after he left that day. I had been hurt by the way he chose to leave me, but I was just as dependent on him as I had ever been. Still, he was spooked once I confessed to my husband. Spooked, but still unwilling to relinquish control. In addition, Maj showed no remorse for everything that I was losing. I cried into the phone one day that I was going to lose my house, and I wouldn't be able to live on Spirit Lake anymore. I was devastated.

"Oh, Talia," Maj sighed over the phone. "Every lake is full of spirit."

Tears poured down my face as I realized that it had all just been a story. Still, I wanted to believe that he *had* cared about me. As he realized that it was going to be difficult and dangerous to continue calling me by phone, he demanded I get a post office box in order to correspond with him. It didn't take me long to realize that it was a sex story, not a love story, that he needed to maintain. He was unwilling to let me go, and he told me so.

When I let Dr. Cole know that I had told my husband the truth, I hoped that he would help me see things clearly, that he would keep his office a safe place for me in the midst of all the turmoil. He did. He also gently suggested that the best way to make Maj take responsibility for the destruction he had brought to my life was to give him nothing in return. No contact. No calls. I expected to have only the help of Dr. Cole, but when I texted Benny that I was getting a divorce he wrote back, "I love you." I didn't know he would be the one to help me pick up all the pieces of both of our broken lives. I only knew that when he said he loved me, I believed him, despite having just been betrayed by someone who began with a claim of love. When I looked into Benny's eyes, I saw a man's burning desire for righteousness and a little boy that wanted love. I saw a poet whose words could swoon any woman off her feet. But God made it clear that he would never let Benny be my savior. We began as friends, but it became impossible not to fall in love. Later, we went into a tattoo shop together, and I watched Benny get a symbol of grace etched into his left arm. He said he had expected to be alone after all he had been through, but then God sent me to him. When it was my turn, I had the tattoo artist cut a lamb into the back of my neck with black ink. As I began to walk into a new life, I continued my journey of recognizing that there was only One who could ever be the sacrificial lamb.

I don't remember the last time I spoke to Maj Ragain. I continued to take his calls for a while. Benny told me that if Maj really loved me, he would take care of me in some way. Offer me the cabin to live in. Something. It was painful to realize that all of his stories, his promises, his professions of love, had been only smoke. He truly was the wolf in sheep's clothing. One day he called, and I didn't answer. Another day he called, and Benny answered, threatening to cripple him worse if he ever called again. He didn't.

We stopped talking, but he was still in my life. He had insisted I remember him, and I found myself doing just that. I realized how badly I had wanted him to be fatherly toward me, to care about the sexual abuse that had taken place, to help me. Dr. Cole helped me see how dangerous it is to keep seeking those unmet, often unconscious, childhood desires. He also helped me to see how common it is for predators to separate the injured from the pack and to prey on them.

The truth is that I actually feared that I was the one abandoning Maj. Then, one day, Dr. Cole sent me a message. "Understand that he is not a victim here. Does he speak for the light and truth with all his words, or is he from the tempter?" I had wanted so badly to resolve the trauma that had taken place, but Maj had every intention of reenacting it instead. From that point on, I trusted

Dr. Cole to look at my unconscious, to see what was broken, and to help me resolve my traumas. He often said that it was as if I had all kinds of internal injuries that were in need of treatment.

In my everyday life, I put one foot in front of the other. Perhaps people saw me and thought I was merely sad because I'd been through a divorce. That couldn't have been further from the truth. I had gone through a divorce in record time, yes, but there were a host of problems before that and a host of problems to follow. My husband was the kindest person to me regarding the divorce. Others in our town looked away from me, gossiped about me, and abandoned me completely. Just before the divorce, I came across a conversation that I was not intended to see in which Benny's ex asked my husband how he could ever forgive me. His reply was, "Because she forgives everybody else."

What my husband lacked in being able to address the issues of my past, he made up for in kindness. As Benny stepped forward to try to help me wade through my difficulties, my husband looked at me one day and said, "I think you two make more sense than we ever did." I'd like to say that I pulled up my bootstraps and became an amazing single mother, but I didn't. I took what my husband said as his blessing and embraced all that Benny offered me, and I did my best to help Benny along the way by listening, loving, and being his best friend. Eventually, beside the waters of another lake, we committed to one another.

Chapter Twenty-Five

*"Will You work wonders for the dead? Shall the dead arise and
praise You? Shall Your lovingkindness be declared in the grave?"
(Psalm 88:10-11)*

In Dr. Cole's office, it was as if I were lying open on an operating
table, completely vulnerable with all of my injuries in full view, and
still bleeding. One day Dr. Cole drew attention to a particular visible
injury.

"Why do you cut on your ankles?" he asked.

I replied that it was an easy place to hide my scars, but he
didn't seem satisfied with that explanation. He suggested that maybe
there was a deeper reason. He explained that he once had a patient
who cut a certain place on his arms but didn't know why. It turned
out that the boy had experienced a painful medical procedure when
he was young, and when he grew older, he began to cut himself
across the arms in the same place where the doctors had strapped
him down. I asked Dr. Cole to tell me what he was telling me. He
had his left leg crossed over his right. He reached down with his
right hand and with his thumb and forefinger pulled on his sock.

I instantly remembered the numerous times that I had told
him that on the night that I had first been raped, I went into the house
with my brother-in-law because he was going to give me socks. This
was only the first of many insights that would help me understand
my injuries and my behavior. For a long time, it felt like Dr. Cole
understood me much better than I did. I told him all my dreams, my
fears, my self-destructive tendencies that threatened to overtake me,
and he offered a calmness that did not change.

For every hour I spent with Dr. Cole, I spent a week with
Benny. I had no place to live, and Benny told me that I could live
with him. He took me to his mom and told her that he loved me. I
immediately thought about how Maj had sent his mother away in
order to "love" me, but Benny took me straight to his mother and
then truly showed me love. That was a lesson to me. Soon, Benny
walked me through the front door of an apartment with a mattress on
the floor. He said I could live there with him and that there was a
room across the hall for my boy. "I want to help you raise your
boy," he said as he ran his fingers through my hair. I looked around
at the tiny apartment, void of color, and felt that perhaps he was

showing me more love than any human being ever had. I accepted
the offer, and his heart. Earlier in the summer, Benny had finished
reading Steinbeck's *East of Eden*, and we both accepted that we
could never be perfect, but that we wanted to be good.

In that apartment, Benny taught me how to eat again. He took
me for breakfast picnics of bagels, cream cheese, and bananas. I later
found out that he had never been a breakfast eater and accused of
him of just wanting to be around a pretty girl first thing in the
morning. He made no argument. We were fiercely codependent. Any
time not spent earning money to survive was spent together. I felt
that I had found the most competent, handsome, intelligent, loving,
man in the world. It was hard to believe that he had suffered as he
had. I was thrilled to introduce my only friend to Dr. Cole, who
smiled and said that he thought we were good for each other. He
later told me privately that he liked Benny, that he was a good guy.

Those three years following my relationship with Maj, the
years following the summer I lost it all, were the hardest of my life.
They were the hardest of Benny's life, too, but he stood by me the
entire way, often putting me before himself. What I wanted most
was to run away from all the damage and destruction of my life and
move forward into a beautiful and pleasant new life, but
unfortunately, that was not the path to my healing. The summer that
I was losing everything was also the summer that Dr. Cole said to
me, "I'd like to try something with you, if you're willing. It's called
exposure therapy."

Exposure therapy involves exposing a patient to their most
fearful experiences in order to help them to overcome their anxieties.
In my case, it would involve rehearsing the details of the night with
my brother-in-law in as much detail as possible. The process helps to
integrate the memory of a traumatic experience and move it from the
working memory--where it can be a constant nuisance--into storage
in long-term memory. It's a difficult and painful process, he told me,
and things often get worse before they get better. All of the thoughts
and feelings that I had been trying to avoid, I now needed to face
head-on, and the mere thought of doing this terrified me. As I cried
at the thought of it, Dr. Cole looked at me sympathetically and said,
"I wish there were a different way, but I think this is what will help."
Trusting Dr. Cole's knowledge and experience, I agreed, and he
taught me ways to cope with the territory we were entering, assuring
me that he knew how hard it would be.

The sessions were recorded, and I listened to them between appointments. The first time I recounted to Dr. Cole the experience of what had happened and how I felt about it took me over forty minutes to complete. The final time I told the story, it took only one minute. Throughout the process, that memory had lost its hold on me, but I still had an incredible amount of work to do. It was still the very early days of my globe being turned upside down. I was suffering whiplash from my sudden divorce. I was nearly friendless. I had started a new job, and Benny and I were living in a two-bedroom apartment with our combined four children, who also were confused and hurt, coming and going from week to week. Watching the pain of our children while we were also suffering was nearly unbearable, and we cried every day. We had moved into this apartment together, out of necessity, because we didn't know what else to do and because we were friends going through the same kinds of problems and falling in love in the process. We jokingly referred to our apartment as our Intensive Care Unit. We were dangerously ill and keeping each other under close observation. It was a tragic, redemptive, ugly, beautiful, love story.

I did keep hold of one friend from the old neighborhood, though. Janet remained a close friend to me throughout my difficult ordeal, though she didn't yet know the circumstances of my divorce. Living on her peaceful point of the lake, a ways down the road from the rest of us, she had been sheltered from much of the gossip that filtered through the air when word spread about my divorce. Janet invited me to her home for a talk, as she often had in the past. She has a Native-American feel to her, with her long dark hair hanging in waves down her back. She is free-spirited and open, and that is always the way I feel when I enter her welcoming home. Her rescued animals scurry around beside her, taking their places on her lap or the chairs beside her. The walls are lined with books that I loved to borrow and discuss with her. Incense rises from the coffee table where it is always burning, filling the air with a sandalwood scent, making smoky concentric circles in the air.

When I went to visit that day, I didn't know that she, too, had injuries from the past to attend. After a few minutes of greeting and catching up, the subject changed to the tremendous upheaval that had taken place in my life. As I sat on her couch looking through the picture window of her living room across the sparkling waters of the lake outside, her eyes found mine and she questioned me in a serious tone about the divorce.

"Did Maj have anything to do with this?"

I was shocked by the direct nature of her question, and by the truth of it. I looked deep into her eyes and replied, "Yes. He had everything to do with this."

"I was afraid of that," she said as she shook her head in sadness. "I had hoped he had moved on from such nonsense."

Upon hearing her response, I was greatly intrigued. I wondered how she had known, without being told, that Maj had contributed to my family falling apart. What followed, as they say, was stranger than fiction. While I had known that Maj and Janet had known each other for many years, I knew nothing of the circumstances of their relationship. I learned that day that decades earlier Janet had been a student of Maj's in the city where he still lived. Maj had taken a liking to her, calling her by a different name than the one that everyone else used for her, just as he had done with me. She told me how Maj had invited "Jane" to his house one evening, and she entered his home that night as a naive, innocent, virgin, but she left as something else.

Eventually, Maj took her back to the cabin on the lake in his hometown, where he lived with her for eight years. She stayed with him through all kinds of addiction, alcoholism, gambling, and infidelity. At the end of those years, she left the chaos of her relationship with Maj and enrolled in nursing school in order to make a better life for herself. She settled into her little house on the lake, just down the road from the cabin where she lived with Maj, and she continues to live there to this day.

Janet had hoped that in the forty years since she was first seduced by Maj that he had settled down. He had married a few times in those years, and Janet still remained in communication with him. She had grown older, and wiser, and she supposed that he must have also learned some hard lessons in life that had caused him to walk a straighter path, but he hadn't. It now made sense to me why Maj was sullen, acting almost like a dog with his tail between his legs, when Janet had visited us the previous summer. Maj had been practicing his cajolery for a very long time, and he didn't want Janet to recognize his game. Janet and I sat as mirror images of each other, finding it difficult to fathom that the same man had seduced us both, that he was in the same business of beguiling vulnerable women over the span of four decades, since he had taken her virginity in his role as her teacher.

We became touchstones for one another that day, allowing each other to make sense of the confusing nature of our experiences with him as we moved forward. Janet is a woman of God. It was our faith that connected us, and I know that nobody could convince either of us that the Spirit of God was not present in each of our conversations and in the healing that took place for both of us.

Chapter Twenty-Six

"If you forgive the sins of any, they are forgiven them."
(John 20:23)

God is the center of this story. He's the center of everyone's story, whether they choose to accept Him or not.

In frustration, Benny had turned his back on God. He said that he had grown tired of seeking after God and declared, "If God really is a Good Shepherd, then He can come and find me." Unsurprisingly, Benny's life fell apart in the years following that statement, but the Faithful Shepherd did find Benny lying face down on a muddy path, crying out for help. That time came for Benny at the same time that he and I met each other, just after I had fallen on my face, too.

Now, Benny was furiously seeking God. I watched as he rose early to read his Bible and prayed on his knees each morning. I, too, was in the process of trying to stand from where I found myself face down in the dirt. Unlike Benny, my faith in God had always been strong. I never stopped believing that God was real, even if it might have seemed to others who were looking at my life from the outside that I was living sinfully. The truth is that I had been seeking God most intensely, searching and reading my entire Bible, during the same year that I had fallen into the trap with Maj, who I had thought was helping me learn and seek of the spiritual things that mattered. No, I never turned my back on God in frustration as Benny had, but I did sin when I had reached for a human hand out of fear rather than trusting in God completely. I had wanted so badly for someone to treat me like a daughter, and that didn't seem like such a bad desire to me. I didn't feel guilty for wanting the love of a father.

In the beginning, Maj had seemed so incredibly safe. How could I, the girl raised in a Christian school who was reading her Bible and going to church every Sunday, not have realized that the fatherly love I was looking for could come only from one person, the Heavenly Father to whom I prayed? Instead, I had become--quite literally--the woman caught in adultery, caught and made to stand before her accusers, and there were stones to be thrown. In my small town, in my church, in my formerly close circles of friends, the stones were raised. Virtually nobody knew the trauma I had encountered at 17 and 21. Some knew that I had struggled with addictions and disordered eating, but nobody knew that Maj had offered his help with these problems. Even I had failed to recognize that I was turning to Maj for something that only God could provide for me.

There was little that I wanted more than to live in a mind that was free of the strongholds that I had constructed from my experiences, strongholds that were built from fear. However, these walls I had built to fortify myself had failed to serve me. In that tiny apartment that Benny and I called the ICU, I realized the tragic truth and daunting task before me. I had to tear down, entirely, all the defensive structures that I had built within myself due to the hurt, anger, and fear I had developed in the traumatic experiences of my past. Filled with regret for even the first brick that was laid, I had to admit that the fortress I had built in order to feel safe, protected, and loved had become a prison from which I could not escape. I had missed the mark. I didn't let the Master Builder build for me. I had tried to do it myself.

Mistakenly, and with all the knowledge I had gained attending Sunday school as a young child and seeking God as an adult, I had taken upon myself the role that Jesus had been given by the Father. I had mistakenly imagined myself as the sacrificial lamb. Though by His wounds I could have been healed, I dragged a razor across my arm in atonement. I had allowed a man to step into the shoes of my Father because I wanted someone I could see and touch and hear to help me through my difficulties. In so doing, I had naively reached for the hand of a man who did not love God. Maj spoke as a prophet and was a dreamer of enchanted dreams, but he did not love God. He loved himself. He wanted to be remembered. That lake ended up being my very own Eden, and I had listened to the flattering words of the tempter.

In the years following my experience with Maj, I went through a variety of emotions regarding my relationship with him. At first, I felt guilty for "abandoning" Maj. Later, I became angry, wondering how someone who had been through multiple affairs and divorces himself could not have known the damage he was doing to my family and relationships by leading me into those circumstances. Finally, I swam through sadness, wondering if Maj had ever really loved me. This was more than a relationship gone bad. The vulnerability I felt as I looked back and realized how Maj had systematically dismantled my defenses was devastating to me. It took a long time to cycle through many different kinds of emotions following my experience with Maj, but eventually I made a purposeful decision to pursue healing. I knew that if I didn't, I would never be able to trust another person again, not even myself.

I was able to open my mind to the possibility of healing, relationships, and trust, but not before I decided to speak to Maj Ragain one last time. I stayed up late one night with all of my confusion and anger, and I wrote until I found forgiveness.

Chapter Twenty-Seven

"Jesus said to him, 'I am the way, the truth, and the life. No one comes to the Father except through Me.'"
(John 14:6)

Sometimes I think about what I learned from you. Again, and again I return to the notion that the wisdom you offered was something I would have been better off to be innocent of. I came to you with a particular kind of innocence. I know now that I was seeking the love of a father. Your age and your physical state provided me with a false sense of safety. The truth was that what you lacked in physical ability you had long ago learned to make up for in the art of manipulation. If I could reclaim something it would be the wisdom of innocence, but that's not available to me.

So, I'll work with what I've got. I'm reminded of the Zen story of the Chinese farmer who did not attribute what looked like a negative situation to bad luck or what appeared to be a positive situation to good luck. The old farmer had learned that there was a greater force behind events. I know this, too. I have strong faith, and you have a keen eye for the faithful, God-fearing woman. You are attracted to it, yet you have a compulsion to destroy it. My faith remains, but my losses were staggering. My faith allows me to know with certainty that the crippling losses that I faced as a result of my involvement with you do not compare to the hope that I have or the good that can be brought out of it.

To be fair, you told me that nobody else would tell me to take the path I was taking with you. You were right. When I uncovered our secret, I lost my husband, half of my precious time with my son, my home, my job, my church and many of my friends. My family stopped talking to me. When I lost the last name that I had shared with my son, I asked my father if he would be okay with me changing my last name to Talia. I think I wanted him to tell me that he wanted me to have his last name. I had just so miserably failed at gaining parental love from you, so I returned to my dad knowing that he was still incapable of providing the acceptance I longed for but hoping he would welcome this prodigal home, even if that acceptance came only in the superficiality of a name. He said, "I don't care what your name is." With a tone of utter disappointment, he said that all he wanted was for me to not have had sex with you. The irony just about did me in. He shook his head and said that he didn't understand how somebody that had been raped could have allowed something like this to happen.

The truth is that it was largely because I had been raped that I allowed this to happen. It's not as if I had mustered up the strength to protect myself against future predators. On the contrary, I was fragile and weak. When you noticed my drastic weight loss, I wrote you that letter, the one revealing the reason for the control issue and self-destruction, the secret behind it: the rape by my sister's fiancé, the man I now have to call my brother. I told you one of the most intimate details of my existence. I didn't know it yet, but you were the wrong person to tell. I wanted to find a new family, and I loved your mom. It didn't work out for me though because the brother I thought I was gaining had sex with me again, and I already knew how that story ended.

I found myself faced with either living the same lie all over again or telling your mother what had happened. I could not bear the thought of burdening her with the truth, nor could I bear the thought of burdening myself with dishonesty any longer, so I let go of her when all I wanted to do was hold on. I abandoned her out of love and a refusal to tarnish what she holds most dear. I let go, lightly. I later found justification and support for what I knew to be true.

Do you remember when you crossed the line? My shrink had just retired suddenly. You asked, "Do you feel abandoned?" The next day as we sat on the dock, you said, "I'm having trouble not being one of the men who wants you." You added that you weren't like the men who had sexually abused me. Then you said, "I want to fuck you once and come in you six times." When you said those words, my mind left my body. I dissociated in order to cope with the threat that you posed. We both know that I could have avoided a lot of hurt by walking away. When I try to recall that memory, I remember it as if I am floating several feet above the dock. I can't remember feeling the planks of the dock beneath me no matter how hard I try. My body may have remained in front of you, but my mind couldn't. Dissociation that powerful also happened at my first appointment with my shrink when I attempted to tell him about the rape that I experienced earlier in my life.

In the moment that you crossed this line, you betrayed any chance of ever actually helping me. Instead of helping me, you terrified me. When I didn't respond receptively, you said, "Do you want me to float away?" I could not fathom how you could threaten to leave me when you knew how horribly abandoned I felt by my psychologist's unexpected retirement. I wasn't yet mature enough to realize that your abandonment of me had already taken place. To further confuse me you said, "I don't know why I said that float away thing. I will never abandon you. I don't know how." And you know, it worked. Knowing that I would never see my shrink again, I became desperate not to feel alone, and I compromised so much more than I could have ever imagined possible. I did tell him, though. I was on my way to my grandfather's graveside service and I called the shrink with the same name as my father and told him exactly what you said. "Damn it, Damn it, Damn it! Why did he have to do this?!" he said. I stood next to my grandfather's grave and typed a text to R, "What is this? Preying on weakness?" He replied, "I'm sorry, yes."

You once told me that you cultivated my naughtiness like a garden of flowers. The analogy of a gardener is good. Gardeners plant a lot of seeds just to see what might sprout up. They pay close attention to the ones that grow. You told me that I was special, but I was just one of many seeds. The circumstances were just right (for you) and a sickly flower of opportunity grew towards you. I wasn't special. I was weak.

I remember you telling me that you used to bang your fists on the steering wheel and cry when you had to drop off your son at your ex-wife's house after spending a weekend with him. It is hard for me to understand how you could never have cared that this would happen to my own child and young family as a result of the perversion you introduced into my life. In the aftermath, I often wondered if you lacked a conscience. In Steinbeck's *East of Eden,* it says that just as physical monsters exist with all types of physical abnormalities, so are mental or psychic monsters born. As a child might go through life without a leg, so might one navigate the world without a conscience. To a monster, the norm would be monstrous, since everyone is normal to himself. At the very least, your conscience is seared. A seared conscience is insensitive to wrongdoing as a result of continually resisting and ignoring its warnings. It becomes numb.

The spiritual-erotic path that you lead me down got awful rocky. I never felt the confidence to openly disagree with you so let me take this opportunity to say that they are not meant to be the same path. The dichotomous path that I followed with you caused extreme dissonance inside of me. The unbridgeable contradiction of your claim to care for me while introducing destruction into my life was too painful to comprehend. The way to care for someone that has been sexually abused is not to have sex with her. Pissing on your hands wasn't going to heal my psychogenic problems. Masturbating wasn't going to serve as a ticket to freedom from my past. My post-traumatic stress would not be helped by an additional injury any more than shooting one of the veteran's in your circle would provide the healing they desire. For these reasons, my journals throughout our relationship can be read as the most obvious form of spiritual warfare. I wanted to do good, but time and time again, I failed. I didn't know then that your son had asked you not to do to me what you had done to so many other women, but I always remember that when he found out that you did he said, "For all your wisdom, magic, and smarts, you sure haven't learned much." I had to come to that conclusion the hard way as well.

Early on, I thought that with your experience you were trying to help me. I believed, like so many others, that you were a wise guru. I thought you'd look out for me. You weren't capable of that, and just as tragically, it doesn't seem like you've learned to do that for yourself. I told you that I heard a voice in my head once when I was looking at you that said, "He'll help." You said it was a daemon. My discernment was diminishing as I interacted with you, and I did not become as frightened by this as I should have. My own conscience was becoming soiled and losing sight of what was suitable and true. You told me that the temptation to trust you came from an evil spirit, and I brushed it off as just another of your imaginary tales. I foolishly missed information that could have provided a way of escape, but instead I rebelliously continued to listen to all that you had to say.

The more that I listened, the more I gained the sense that you didn't think the abuse I suffered sexually was very serious. This culminated when you raised your voice at me on the phone one afternoon saying, "You have a past! So what? A priest tried to suck my cock when I was in the hospital as a child! I kicked him and told him to go away, so he moved on to the next kid and I got over it!" I was never able to see that event in your life as a trivial encounter. While I silently empathized with this briefly mentioned trauma from your past, you encouraged me to take sex lightly and admonished me for using phrases like "hit on" to describe men's flirtation or pursuit of me, pointing out that it was not as if I was hurt by their advances. I came across something entitled "A Narcissist's Prayer" that accurately depicts the progression that took place from me telling you that I was misused sexually to you becoming the one to misuse me. The prayer goes, "That didn't happen. And if it did, it wasn't that bad. And if it was, that's not a big deal. And if it is, that's not my fault. And if it was, I didn't mean it. And if I did, you deserved it."

You gaslighted me, constantly telling me that the dimmed lights were bright. You repeatedly rewrote history with untruths that were always in your favor. I did not seduce you. I didn't paddle over and offer myself to you. Your long con was much more organized and methodical than I ever could have recognized, being 44 years behind in experience. The first time you told me to take my clothes off, you laughed about the fact that my facial expression and body language screamed that I didn't want to do it while I obeyed each instruction you gave. Every act of obedience towards you was an act of disobedience for which I am responsible. I was not, in the chaos of my mind, yearning for a chance to touch myself and provide you with a taste of me.

You prefer to live in a world of enchantment and myth. You told me that I was the beguiling one, though this only further epitomized your own deception. When a thief sees a holy man, he sees only his pockets, right? You couldn't afford me, but you took me anyway. If there is a lesson love should teach us it is this: give, don't take. While I no longer ascribe our coming together as a beautiful, preordained "fault in our stars," I do believe in synchronicity and that God sends prophets and help in our time of need. One came to Jawbone. You asked him to read a poem to drive out the devil and he read "White Man." The prophet would later reappear on your doorstep, urging you to turn from your destruction, but you persisted. I think you are a prophet, too. I read about you. I read that there were false prophets who secretly bring in damnable ideas that deny faith, even denying God. They bring destruction on themselves and many follow their insidious ways. Through covetousness they make merchandise of others with feigned words. You see, their judgment has long been idle, and their damnation doesn't sleep. They are presumptuous and self-willed. As brute beasts, they speak evil of things they do not understand, and they perish in their own corruption. They have eyes full of adultery and they cannot cease from sin. They beguile unstable souls. Forsaking the right path, they go astray and ignore the promptings of true prophets. They are wells without water. Speaking with great swelling words of vanity, they allure through the lusts of the flesh those that were clean. These prophets promise freedom, but they are servants of corruption. For those that were living in innocence, it would have been better for them not to become entangled with the false prophet. I should never have turned from my path to yours.

Near the end, you screamed at me, "Everywhere I go, I can't walk! Everywhere I go, I can't breathe!" I have wondered if you wished for me to be paralyzed with you. I wore a bracelet in your presence once that said, *Talitha koum*. Translation: "Rise up little girl and walk." You said, "Please, don't." You can no longer climb the stairs to the prostitute, but you can pull a damaged girl to your mat. For a long time after you, everywhere I went, I could not trust. Even my dreams, which you were always so interested to hear, remind me of the danger I encountered. I've become a more skilled dreamcatcher than when you knew me. I had a dream that I was standing in a field and a fox approached me. "Is that a snake?" I asked. I then drew a picture so I could warn others of what I'd seen. I drew a sloth. My dream posed a riddle. What's cunning like a fox, crafty like a snake and slow like a sloth? You. You enter as a wise old fox but are craftier than any of the beasts in the field, and you can't hide that nature of the snake that is in you for long. To protect others, I will share the knowledge of evil that I have acquired. I am now aware that an exploiter can appear harmless and slow-moving. It is, in fact, the gradual nature of the deception that renders it difficult to identify. I had a "gift of fear" within me, but I did not trust my intuition because I had decided to trust you. My eyes are now opened.

When I cut ties with you, I missed something that I never found in the first place. The last time I saw you, I buttoned your denim shirt and rolled up the cuffs of your sleeves for you. After fulfilling every sexual favor you had asked of me for the week of your stay in the cabin, pouring the piss from your Mason jars and dressing you for your journey back to Ohio, you looked at me and said, "Go home." I hugged you, and you gave nothing in return. You mentioned later that maybe your coldness towards me was the reason I uncovered our secret. It wasn't. Someone who had turned from his sin had entered both my life, and by extension, yours. The same prophet that urged you to turn from error suggested that I be honest and allow my husband the knowledge of what he was choosing each day when he chose me. I told you that when you showed me the best and worst parts of yourself, I chose both. My husband did not choose both, and he deserved the respect of making an informed decision. I regret that in accepting the worst, monstrous parts of you, I became a monster to my husband and to your wife. Benny and I were able to acknowledge the worst parts of one another and help each other turn from them so that we could enjoy and choose the best parts of ourselves and offer them to the other.

You suggested that when you were gone from this world, I should write your name and put it in a bottle to toss into the river. You told me that as an old woman I would look up into the sunshine streaming through the trees and think of you. I will remember you, that's true. I'm sure you recall that I started treatment with a Dr. Cole near the end of our relationship. A couple of weeks ago he came across that same story of the false prophet. He thought of you. Your legacy is carried with me.

I burned your books, but they are rife with confessions of your immorality and corruption, overlooked by those still focused on your charm and blinded by their pity. I implore you to consider the book that Dr. Cole and I read from. It provides a mirror for you to look into and the chance to change what you see. With it, holy the firm is comprehensible. Consider why the faith-filled girl next door would ask this of you. I'll leave you now with all I have to offer, my forgiveness, God's love, and God's Word. You once said that I was forgiving you even as you harmed me. That was not true. I'm forgiving you now. I wrote in one of my journals that you told me that the final fruit of God's love is forgiveness. Actually, He allowed us to be born through the Word of Truth, that we should be a kind of first fruits of all that He created. It is not forgiveness but the cross of Christ that is the final fruit of God's love. If you accept His forgiveness and his final fruit, your death can be life.

-- Talia

Chapter Twenty-Eight

"Instead of your shame you shall have double honor."
(Isaiah 61:7)

The next morning, I wrote Maj's address on the center of an envelope and stamped it with enough postage to carry my letter of forgiveness on a 500-mile journey. As I dropped the envelope into the blue, out of town, mailbox at the post office, every memory I ever had of my time with him flashed through my mind. After, I walked into Dr. Cole's office for my weekly appointment, holding a second copy of the letter in my hand.

"You were suggesting a catharsis of sorts, weren't you?" I asked him.

For some time, Dr. Cole had been suggesting that I might be able to find a way of transition that would enable me to free myself from the torment of Maj's psychological grip.

"I did it," I said.

I read him the letter I had written for Maj that was filled with fifteen years of repressed emotion and suffering from all the abuses I experienced from him and other men. After reading the last line of the letter, I looked to him for approval.

"Beautiful," he said. "You should go look in the mirror."

I looked at him hesitantly.

"Go to the bathroom and look at yourself," he entreated me.

Standing to my feet, I left the comfortable chair in Dr. Cole's office, walked into the hallway, and turned the corner to the women's restroom. Pulling back a bandana that covered my hair, I stared at my reflection in the bathroom mirror to find the beauty that Dr. Cole had recognized, and I noticed that my eyes lacked the torment that had been present in them for far too long. Instead, my forehead was smooth, and my cheeks and mouth showed no sign of tension.

I returned to his office and sat down.

"Did you see it?" he asked, with a smile.

It was impossible not to smile back at him. "I'm relaxed."

I never expected to hear back from Maj. He didn't respond to the letter, but only a few days after sending it, I did hear from him. While watching videos posted on the Internet, I happened upon a video of him reading some of his new poems publicly, at a cafe. On the video, after being praised as a good friend to many and a native of my hometown, Maj accepted a warm round of applause and began reading a poem titled "Rogue Wave in the Rosebushes." Like all of Maj's poetry, the seemingly beautiful language does much to leave his audience captivated. With the knowledge and hurt that I now carried, I knew how unsightly the story was. It was obvious that the poem was written about his wife finding out about his infidelity with me, though it would be impossible for any of his readers to understand the truth of this since he had kept the secrets of his life hidden from them. In the poem, he refers to a rosebush that snaps back and cuts into his wife's cheek with its thorns. I remembered one of his nicknames for me: *Rosebud.* Dismissive of his wife's pain, he tells her to leave it all behind and suggests that they spray paint the words "Jesus loves me" on his mom's Oldsmobile now that she's in the nursing home.

As the video continues, he reads several more poems from the anthology of his life's work. Some are old, but many are new. Now cognizant of the secrets of his hidden life, I could see more clearly the infidelities of previous relationships expressed in poems he had composed before he had met me. It seemed I had become one more trophy along the way, one more poem to add to his books. At the end of the video, he closes with a poem called "The Brief Life of Honeysuckle." That brief life is mine.

He takes a deep breath and brings his hand to his face to scratch his mustache and hide his dishonesty before a pained look comes across his face and he begins reading. Disguised in words that suggest he is reminiscing about a fishing trip to Spirit Lake, he reads a poem about me, my body, how he sexualized me, and how he lost me. As the poem comes to an end, he speaks:

> *On the way back to the dock, the words of the prophet Muhammad came back to me. He said: "God has made a polish for everything that tarnishes and the polish for the heart is remembrance." What brushed past me this evening?*

With a shaking hand and a downturned face, he finishes:

> *That dark wing polishes my heart, even now.*

Later, I learned that the prophet Muhammad had taken a child as a bride. Aisha was 44 years younger than Muhammad, just as I am 44 years younger than Maj Ragain. Some synchronicities are heart-wrenching. I was so disgusted by the poem and how he could completely disregard the pain he had caused me and continue to believe that what had happened between us was good as long as he *remembered* everything about it. I was so frustrated at the thought that I didn't catch the message given to me in the very last line of his poem. I woke up the next morning, with the phrase *the bird is on the wing* running through my half-conscious mind. Then, it came to me. It was a line from a poem he shared with me very early in our relationship, an excerpt from *The Rubaiyat of Omar Khayyam*. This was only one of the many times that my unconscious memory came to my aid in order to show me just how severe his manipulation of me had been. The final stanza of his poem expressed his unrepentant heart. He hadn't cared that he hurt me.

Within months of receiving my letter, Maj released a new book. *Clouds Pile up in the North* contains both of the poems about me that I heard him reading on the Internet that day, and it is filled with innuendoes that Benny and I can hear and see as clearly as if Maj were telling the truth. He doesn't, of course, tell the truth, but I see my story throughout his book. In fact, Benny's name is also in the title poem of the book. "Brave Benny" is an ant that is dropped to the concrete and stepped on by a size-four Batman tennis shoe, footwear that Maj imagined to be worn by my toddling son. The cover of the book features a painting of the dock that will forever remain in my memory, the place where he took advantage of all that was going wrong in my life for his own personal gain. The book is a testimony of his conquest of me, just as I am sure that many of his previous books of poetry have been testaments of conquests for other women he has used.

Far from being sorry, Maj is proud of his conquests, and when he reads his poems to his audiences, he gets to relive the experiences in memory. Maj's poetry mirrors the behavior of a serial killer who keeps a trophy from his victims. A lock of hair or a piece of jewelry helps prolong, even nourish, the fantasy of the crime. Maj's poems are like newspaper clippings that allow him to remember the crimes he committed, and how he got away.

Chapter Twenty-Nine

"But He was wounded for our transgressions, He was bruised for our iniquities; the chastisement for our peace was upon Him, and by His stripes we are healed."
(Isaiah 53:5)

Rape is a killer of many, many things. It murders choice, control, and agency. It threatens self-esteem, and it leaves its victim a collapsible version of herself. I sometimes considered what my suicide might accomplish. I imagined my death as a note to my family regarding what had taken place with my brother-in-law. I wanted my dead body to say, "I was telling the truth." Maybe the man from the hotel would remember what he'd done to me as he read my obituary. I considered that maybe Maj would hear me saying, "You should repent," from my grave.

But mostly, I wished for death because I wanted my torment to end.

I came to Dr. Cole because I couldn't stop playing with death like a toy in my hands. I asked Benny to put me out of my misery more than once. Both of these men sat with me in my darkness and pain, rather than attempting to rush me through to a place of light. I will forever see their acceptance of my suffering as a great act of kindness and patience. It was the groundwork for helping me to become capable of change. As a result of their kindness, I was able to learn that while disappointment and abuse occur in relationships, so does healing.

I often wonder how long the woman caught in adultery continued to stand before Jesus after He said, "Neither do I condemn you, go and sin no more," before she was able to comprehend his words. The week that I wrote and read my letter, Jesus's words finally sunk in for me.

Jesus had never asked me to suffer in condemnation and shame. My pain of being raped had been ignored, denied, and even exploited. Many stones had been raised against me, but my own unforgiveness was the stone that I needed to release. After I had forgiven Maj, I was able to work backwards and come to a place of forgiveness for the other men who had used me wrongly. I no longer wanted to kill myself after I had become able to forgive. My suicidal thoughts had only been misplaced anger, turned inward, toward myself. After a fifteen-year struggle with alcohol, I was able to stop drinking and stay sober. One day, after entering Dr. Cole's office, he said that he noticed something different about me. Unsure of what he could be noticing, I asked for clarification.

"Today is the first time that I've seen joy in your eyes. The entire time you've been coming here, even your micro-expressions have communicated sadness."

I had been seeing Dr. Cole for three years at this point. "I haven't looked happy for three years?" I asked him, incredulously.

"No, you haven't," he replied empathetically.

The word patient means "one who suffers." I was most certainly Dr. Cole's patient, but as he has pointed out many times, I also have a Master Shrink who is willing to heal. Weeping has endured throughout many of the painful experiences of my life, but joy has grown, too, as I have come to understand what it meant for Christ to *despise* the shame of the cross. I had never properly understood what it meant to *despise* something. I had grown up thinking that despising something meant to hate it with great intensity. I have since learned that this word may be better understood as meaning to regard something with contempt because it has no value. Just as Jesus regarded the shame of the cross as having no value when compared against the riches of heavenly glory, I know that whatever shame I may have endured in the past is also worthless in comparison to the eternal joy He has promised. Still, this anticipation of joy is mingled with sorrow.

The process of facing devastating abuse and sorting through my self-destructive behavior has been difficult. I have experienced a lot of anger and grief along the way. When I came to understand that I could never find a better way to heal than to trust in the Lamb that God had sent to bear my suffering and shame better than I ever could, I began to experience moments of joy. No, I did not arrive at a complete epiphany of joy all at once. Rather, I live each day moment by moment in a state of joyful sorrow. I have no expectation that I will ever be completely free from the pangs of grief in this life. After all, Jesus promised, "In the world you will have tribulation, but be of good cheer; I have overcome the world" (John 16:33). Whatever pain and distress I may have endured through my own sins or the sins of others have already been borne by my Savior. As I came to understand this more fully, old familiar passages from the Bible came to life for me, and I was able to accept that He bore my suffering so that I could have peace. I embraced His healing.

All along, Maj had wanted me to reject feelings of shame, to snuff out my conscience in order to allow him to do whatever his flesh wanted. He urged me to accept what was meant to be, reminding me that all he had to give to me would find me. What Maj meant to give to me was not meant to be. Maj spoke in order to turn me away from God, but God had planted something different in me long before Maj did. My faith had been given to me as a gift from my Heavenly Father, and it could not be destroyed.

Afterword

"If your hand or your foot causes you to stumble, cut it off and throw it from you; it is better for you to enter life crippled or lame, than to have two hands or two feet and be cast into the eternal fire."
(Matthew 18:8)

Imagine the lowest moment of your life. Perhaps a time you were committing a sin or being abused. See Jesus hanging on the cross for you at that exact same moment in time. Accepting this will change your life. I see myself on a cabin floor, submitting my body and mind to evil and saying with my actions that God was not enough. I see Him protecting my soul from the torment my body and mind endured. I no longer have to feel guilty for what happened with my brother-in-law. I do not have to berate myself for not understanding how to protect myself from the men who came after him. I can let go of every repugnant memory made behind that hotel room door. From my experiences with Major Ragain, I can go forth wise as a serpent but innocent as a dove.

As I write these words, it has been four years since I lost everything but my faith in God. Janet contacted me last summer to tell me that the cabin was being torn down. We went into it together one last time and prayed before it was demolished. My friend, Maj's mother, passed away on a September day, one day after Maj's birthday. Maj died seven months later.

Just as he always asked me, I will continue to remember Maj Ragain. I dream about him often. My mind is filled with memories of his presence and our many conversations. The first time I ever wrote to Maj, he was right across the yard. He'd dropped many hints that he would appreciate me writing to him. I sat at my dining room table and spent an hour constructing a letter to him. To this day, I am shocked at what I communicated. I wrote to him about the paralytic man in the book of Mark. Looking back, I can't believe that I called such attention to his physical condition so early in our relationship. I remember thinking that I was simply sharing with him what I happened to be studying and learning at the time and that I couldn't help it if there was a bit of a coincidence when it came to the fact that the man in the story could not walk. I focused heavily on the fact that Jesus healed the spiritual before the physical. I did not know at the time that Maj did not believe in God. I wonder now what reaction he had to excerpts like,

> *Which is easier: to say to this paralyzed man, "Your sins are forgiven," or to say, "Get up, take your mat and walk?"*

There seems to be a sweet spot when it comes to the perception of difficult circumstances in our lives. When you are too close or too far away from something, you risk not seeing the picture clearly. As I was living through these events, I was unaware of unconscious motivations, blinded by deception, and unable to grasp the meaning of all that was taking place. Other people were just far enough from me that they were unable to see clearly what was happening to me or offer any help. While my family members certainly fit into this category, I have grown to better understand the difficulties that they faced as well. My sister is kind and faithful. We have an eternal friendship, regardless of the burdens of this life. Both of my parents love me, and it is because of their expressed faith and love for God that I was able to meet the difficulties in my life armed with the truth. They have my heartfelt gratitude and love.

With God's help, Benny and I are rebuilding our lives together. He became an ordained minister and I became a licensed mental health counselor. We live with Abram in a small house on a different lake. I continue to see Dr. Cole every week.

As for Maj, I don't know what decision he ultimately made regarding faith in God. But in my dreams, he walks.

THE END

Other titles from Higher Ground Books & Media:

Wise Up to Rise Up by Rebecca Benston

A Path to Shalom by Steen Burke

Overcomer by Forrest Henslee

Miracles: I Love Them by Forest Godin

Out of Darkness by Stephen Bowman

Dear You by Derra Nicole Sabo

I Don't Want to Be Like You by Maryanne Christiano-Mistretta

Shameless Persistence by Sandra Bretting

Jack Kramer's Journey by Frank Adkins

Chronicles of a Spiritual Journey by Stephen Shepherd

The Real Prison Diaries by Judy Frisby

The Silent Destruction by Yasmin S. Brown

Add these titles to your collection today!

http://www.highergroundbooksandmedia.com

Do you have a story to tell?

Higher Ground Books & Media is an independent Christian-based publisher specializing in stories of triumph! Our purpose is to empower, inspire, and educate through the sharing of personal experiences.

Please visit our website for our submission guidelines.

http://www.highergroundbooksandmedia.com

www.ingramcontent.com/pod-product-compliance
Lightning Source LLC
LaVergne TN
LVHW011353080426
835511LV00005B/274